YORKSHIRE & LINCOLNSHIRE

Edited by Donna Samworth

First published in Great Britain in 2002 by
YOUNG WRITERS
Remus House,
Coltsfoot Drive,
Peterborough, PE2 9JX
Telephone (01733) 890066

HB ISBN 0 75434 010 4
SB ISBN 0 75434 011 2

FOREWORD

This year, Young Writers proudly presents a showcase of the best short stories and creative writing from today's up-and-coming writers.

We set the challenge of writing for one of our four themes - 'General Short Stories', 'Ghost Stories', 'Tales With A Twist' and 'A Day In The Life Of . . .'. The effort and imagination expressed by each individual writer was more than impressive and made selecting entries an enjoyable, yet demanding, task.

Write On! Yorkshire & Lincolnshire is a collection that we feel you are sure to enjoy - featuring the very best young authors of the future. Their hard work and enthusiasm clearly shines within these pages, highlighting the achievement each story represents.

We hope you are as pleased with the final selection as we are and that you will continue to enjoy this special collection for many years to come.

CONTENTS

Amotherby CP School, Malton

Bobby Leach	1
Lydia Spencer	2
Fiona Marsden	3
Amy Burnett	4
Bryony Goddard	5
Jessica Drew	6

Ancaster CE Primary School, Grantham

Rowan Walsh	7
Bethan Watson	8
Claudia Kerr	9
Jacob Storey	10
Lauren Cook	11
Heather Nugent	12
James Taylor	13

Carr Lane Junior School, Willerby

Phillip Best	14
Matthew Ives	15
Sarah Whitham	16
Lauren Haley	17
Selesha Flanagan	18
Sean Meek	19
Abbie Kirk	20
Daniel Thirkettle	21
Victoria Brown	22
Dominic Young	23
James Milestone	24
Rachel Key	25
Andrew Hancocks	26
Rebecca Gilson	27
Raine Partis	28
Ryan Hall	29
Joseph Cooper	30

David Skelton	31
Jayne Witherwick	32
Nicky Rudd	33
Stacey Roche	34
Jack Reger	35
Lucy Henderson	36
Matthew Chester	38
Rachel Kendall	39
Victoria Hussey	40
Jamie Young	41
Lucy Baker	42
Hannah Cooper	43
Emily Petch	44
Scott Annandale	45
Imogen Mercer Swain	46
Nick Johnson	47
Mark Cressey	48
Alex Edge	49
Callum Williams	50
Dawn Gray	51

Crowle County Primary School, Nr Scunthorpe

Josh Simpson	52
Kirsty Bowles	53
Sophie Colebrook	54
Kit Rawlings	55
Samantha Stephens	56
Graeme Fletcher	57
Chloe Stuart	58
Sarah Kitching	59
John Robinson	60
Lewis Arrand	61
Louise Ella	62
Karl Goulding	63
Sophie Grimbleby	64
Kieran Simpson	65

Helpringham Primary School, Nr Sleaford

Gareth Ambler 66
Oliver Jones 67
Alec Vickerson 68
Jack Musson 69
Sophie Hurley 70
Joanna Fihelebon 71
Jacob Wright 72
Abigail Jones 73
Joseph Spencer 74
Kathryn Herbert 75
Robert Spencer 76
Sophie Floyd 78
Katie Prince 79

Lord Deramore's Primary School, York

Liam Summers 80
Angus Vasili 81
Itamar Lavidor 82
Yasha Tchetchik 83
Sophie Wright 84
Christopher Whiting 85
Lucie Berry 86
Adam McMahon 87
Charlotte Cooper 88
Dean Dunn 89
Jodie Ridsdale 90
Thomas Johnson 91
Lauren Beadnell 92
Rachel Lovelady 93
Jordan Coulson 94
Kimberley Bostock 95
Amy Muckersie 96
Faye Garland 97
Natalie Clarke 98
Rebekah Hattee 99
Lorna Stillie 100
Scott Sellars 102

Busi Moon 103
Greg Lawn 104
Jasmine Tubridy 105
Gavin Himsworth 106
Lucy Thompson 107
Hannah Dolling 108
Maahvash Hassib 109
David Crawshaw 110

Nafferton Primary School, Driffield
Ian Dawson 111
Terri Gascoigne 112
David Lund 113
Elizabeth Taysom 114
Joel Westaway 115
Harry Holmes 116
Claire Woodmansey 117
Laurie Glover 118

St Vincent's RC Primary School, Hull
Francesca Seetal 119
Ellis Todd 120
James Wilson 121
Thomas Salisbury 122
Rónan James Burns 123
Emily Rowson 124
Robert Murray 125
Becky Anholm 126
Laurence Harwood 127
Liam Carpenter-Robson 128
Thomas Trewhitt 129
Charlie Haite 130
Callum McLeod 131
Sean Anholm 132
Nancy Hawksworth 133
Stephanie Fish 134
Alistair Bromyard 135
Leon Martin 136

Christopher Hopkin	137
Oliver Dolphin	138
Elena Prosser	139
Claire Medina	140
Connor Cheesman	141
Beth Mulchinock	142
Shaka Cooper	143
Lydia Coyle	144
Emma Wilson	145
Adam Keech	146
Louise Wilson	147
Paige Boxshall	148
Emily Stout	149
Charlotte Lee	150

Scarcroft Primary School, York

Ryan Ellerby	151
Molly Crosland	152
Eleanor Rushton	153
Jonathan Burr	154
Fred Woodcock	155

Snaith Primary School, Nr Goole

Daniel Lemmon	156
Marie Moles	157
Jacob Puckering	158
Sophie Gardner	159
Sarah McGuinness	160
Jack Wilson	161
Nicholas Moore	162
Emily Carey	164
Hannah Bartle	165
Jonathan Crossley	166
Edward Coulden	167
Jasmine Wright	168
Rebecca Watts	169
Flora Squire	170
Stephanie Wade	171

Faye Brignall 172
Amy Hardy 173
Kelly Taylor 174
Matthew Smith 175
Lucy Walton 176
Rachael Grimes 177
Jessica Bridge-Dunk 178
Ryan Garbett 179
Megan Flanagan 180
Mathew Hobson 181
Lucy Baker 182
Daniel Hill 183
Tim Rooker 184
Samantha West 185
Oliver McArdle 186
Zoë Bakewell 187
Faye Bowmer 188
Poppy Robinson 189

Swineshead St Mary's Primary School, Boston
Stephanie Hill 190

The Stories

Castle Nightmare

One late warm Wednesday evening, I was walking home from football practise when all of a sudden I heard a *bloodcurdling scream!* It was coming from the horizon by the old castle.

The next day, after school, me and Frazier went down the lane to the path which lead to the castle. We started to walk down the path, my knees were trembling and I could tell Frazier's were too. We reached the castle and walked to the door. There was a gargoyle on one of the spires. On the door was a stone head.

I opened the door, *creak* flew out of the rusty hinges. We took a few steps in when I saw a shadow appear and ever so quickly disappear.
'Frazier, I just saw a shadow.'
'You're just imagining things.'
'Am I? Because I just saw it again over there!'
'No you didn't!'
'OK.'
'There it *is!'*
'Where?'
'There!'
'Ahhh!'

We ran out and hid behind a bush. The thing came out, it was actually Jake in a suit. We shouted, 'Hey Jake, what were you doing?'
'Just playing.'
'Just playing. You almost scared us to death!'

Me, Frazier and Jake walked home in silence.

Bobby Leach (9)
Amotherby CP School, Malton

ANOTHER DAY IN THE LIFE OF A CAT

It was 6.00am when I came in from hunting that night. I was exhausted so I had my cat food and got in my basket. I'd been trying to catch the same rat for nights and still hadn't caught it.

At 8.00am I woke up and had a wash! I prowled downstairs to see if there was any milk left from the children's cereal, but they had toast and they don't put milk on their toast. (I thought it would taste nice but I don't think they thought it would.) I went to see if there was any milk in my dish but there wasn't, not even any biscuits.

At 12.00pm I gave myself another wash after having another lay down. I just remembered it was Sunday and every Sunday they have chicken! I pounced into the kitchen feeling happy. My owner gave me lots of chicken and a bowl of creamy milk. I purred as I lapped my milk.

At 3.00pm I woke up from my long nap and had a stretch. I had a long think on how to catch the rat and eventually got a purr-fect idea! I would pretend I was asleep and when the rat comes past I will pounce!

Later that very night I set myself up. I saw the rat coming, I pounced and caught it. But when I looked, it was just a pile of leaves but there was something inside. It was a massive rat! So I *had* caught one after all!

Lydia Spencer (9)
Amotherby CP School, Malton

Twin Trouble!

It was Monday morning. The twins, Harry and Henry, were getting ready for school. Harry was always very tidy and organised, but Henry was the complete opposite - he was lazy and uninteresting.

'Hurry up Henry!' called Mum. 'It's your turn to pack the school bags!' 'I'm coming,' muttered Henry. He took his time going down the stairs, trying hard to be awkward.

Eventually he arrived in the kitchen and started to pack his and his brother's school bags. First the homework went in, then the reading books, then the pack-ups, and last of all, the glasses. Henry knew that he had made a mistake somehow, but he didn't know what. He decided not to bother because they had to catch the bus.

At school Harry and Henry sat next to each other. Once they had got their books out and handed their homework in, they got their glasses out. The twins put them on, and suddenly they were in a different world. The teacher was a big, green, hairy monster and the other children were like mini vampires. The tables and chairs were floating in mid-air like islands in the sea.

When they got to lunch the dinner ladies were like Draculas and the teacher on duty was a zombie. Harry and Henry were terrified, but they didn't say anything incase they offended someone.

When they got home their Mum, who looked like a Cyclops, told them to take their glasses off. Suddenly everything was back to normal again. Then they realised that they had put on the wrong glasses and laughed until their stomachs hurt. After they had described their day to Mum, she giggled for a while too.

It had been a very busy day, but when the twins went to bed they were still sniggering.

Fiona Marsden (10)
Amotherby CP School, Malton

A Tale With A Twist

'Oh no!' Suzi cried.
'What? What?' I said, looking around.
'It's the school bullies - Sydney, Ben and Leo!' she moaned. 'Quick, down this alleyway.'

Panting, we rounded a corner. I spotted a derelict house. With the bullies behind us, I pulled Suzi into a bush and I climbed a tall oak tree.

As I climbed down from the tree I heard Suzi shout, 'Quick, over here. The door's open.'

I scrambled down from the tree, unfortunately fell, skidded in some mud and tumbled into the house. The door slammed shut behind me.

'What's it like in there?' called Suzi.
'Pretty dark!' I called back. I took a step forward and suddenly the lights blared on. As I blinked in the bright light, I saw that the house was decorated with balloons and streamers. A birthday party, of course, it was my birthday. A chorus of 'Happy birthday' arose and my friends tumbled down to me. I sat down to enjoy a birthday feast fit for a king. (I wouldn't give it to him for anything though!)

Amy Burnett (11)
Amotherby CP School, Malton

Squirrel's New Home

Rain poured down, lightning ripped the sky into pieces and thunder crashed so loudly that it seemed to poor Squirrel, cowering in his tree, that someone was throwing heavy furniture about in the sky. A sudden instinct told Squirrel to run, and he did, moments before lighting struck the tree and it fell with a deafening crash which shook the ground for miles around, miles of mud caked earth with a complete lack of trees.

Crouching under a bush, Squirrel waited for the storm to end. As the first silver fingers of the dawn brushed the Earth, Squirrel rose and headed to the north at a steady pace. Hours later, muddy and weary, Squirrel stopped to feast on berries from a bush he had reached. Five minutes later Squirrel stopped in disbelief. It couldn't be a treetop there, on the horizon!

Eagerly he scampered forwards and saw . . . a forest! Joyfully Squirrel scampered among the trees, and he soon found the perfect home. When Squirrel reached the top of the tree he stared in wonder, for on the topmost branch sat the most beautiful lady squirrel he had ever seen.

When his wife, the lady squirrel, gave birth, Squirrel was the happiest creature alive.

Bryony Goddard (11)
Amotherby CP School, Malton

THANK GOD FOR TREES

Ruby clumped into the playground in her bright green silicone heels. Stamping to her favourite tree, she leant against it, sighing mournfully.

That Daphne! And Evadne was almost as bad! Daphne always copied her work, whatever the subject, and if she was in a really malicious mood, she would call to the teacher, 'Miss, Ruby's been copying my work!' She's written exactly the same!'

Just at that moment Antonia joined her. They had just begun a plan of action (Ruby v Daphne) when they saw Daphne herself, advancing. Quickly, they swung up the tree to a large, hidden fork where they hid.

Daphne and Evadne stopped just below them. 'I'll deal with Ruby!' they heard Daphne whisper.
'And I'll take Antonia,' Evadne replied. 'What's the plan anyway?'

Ruby looked back at Antonia. She was writing everything down, her eyes gleaming.

'I've found a way to eavesdrop on their mobiles!' Daphne continued. 'They must have said some stuff about us. We'll erase parts about our copying, and give it to Miss Smithson. It can't fail!'

'Oh, I assure you it can!' cried Ruby. 'Get this to Miss Smithson, quick! And thank God for trees!'

Jessica Drew (11)
Amotherby CP School, Malton

A Day In The Life Of Hermione Granger

I woke up and realised I was late for Charms. 'Oh no!' I said in a horror-struck voice. 'What will Professor Flitwick say?'

I quickly got dressed and rushed to the Charms classroom. Three minutes later I arrived and looked at my watch. 'Oh good,' I said breathing heavily. I wasn't late after all; it must have been my clock. I opened the door and walked in, sat at a desk and dropped my bag.

Ten minutes later other people started coming in and doing the same as me, then Professor Flitwick arrived and stood on a pile of books. Then he taught us to make objects, like feathers, float in the air.

Later, I entered Arithmancy, where we multiplied numbers and added them on again, which was very easy. And then I came out ten minutes later to go for a walk. Next I went to the Great Hall for dinner, which was shepherd's pie, which exploded as soon as you bit into it, and delicious cherry trifle for dessert. After that I went to bed, feeling somehow satisfied after a long day.

Rowan Walsh (9)
Ancaster CE Primary School, Grantham

A Day In The Life Of Nina (Cat)

'Let me in!' I yelled in my high voice, as I scratched the glass patio door with my lethal claws and miaowed! My faithful owner, Bethan, came and opened the door to let me in.

Wow, a new fluffy toy! As I brushed against Bethan's legs to say thank you, she patted my head and kissed me saying, 'Good boy Nina.'

Then I followed Bethan into the lounge and was excited about my new toy. It was out of its packet and ready to be played with. As this green fluffy object went over my head, I jumped and grabbed it. I plucked the green feathers out and started licking them, which tasted good, like the last blackbird I had eaten, which my master told me off for, for being a nasty kitty!

By this time I felt hungry for some Whiskas and started miaowing for some dinner. Ding, ding, ding! I heard my dish rattling and started to run. I woofed my delicious food down me and yawned, showing all my gleaming teeth, and walked toward my basket, laid down and closed my eyes. I felt in my dreams a kiss on my sweet little head.

Bethan Watson (11)
Ancaster CE Primary School, Grantham

A DAY IN THE LIFE OF SPUD

I woke up one Saturday morning with the sun shining on me like a newly sprouted sunflower. I plodded over to my water bowl and lapped the water. I sat down and waited for something exciting to happen, but nothing did so I explored the house. I looked in every room.

I eventually found something to do. It was the cat, Kit. He groomed his coat. It reminded me of a bat scrawling across the thick black sky. He realised that it was me and dashed down stairs with me running after him. He stopped and spat at me. I growled and barked at him. He leapt on the work surface and jumped out of an open window. I ran to the back door and dived through the cat flap.

I proudly trotted to my itching spot and rolled on the grass. My friend, Charlie, came out from the back door and sniffed around and ambled back inside. He was always dopey and hungry. My master called me to come in, I ran to the back door.

With the summer's air blowing in my face and the smell of grass cuttings, I went to bed and fell fast asleep.

Claudia Kerr (10)
Ancaster CE Primary School, Grantham

A Day In The Life Of Me

It was lunchtime on Wednesday the 22nd of May. The rest of the maths challenge team and I shot off to collect two other members. Then, off to St George's College of Technology, where we were welcomed with refreshments.

The quiz started shortly after. We got off to a flying start with all correct in the first round, and full marks in the speed round.

Eventually we won! It was totally, amazingly brilliant. We won a scientific calculator for each member and collected the St George's Maths Quiz trophy. We were going to be in the local newspaper as well. The photographer took our names then photographed us with Tom Prosser holding the trophy. It felt good.

When I got home I felt proud, and so did my mum when I told her. I told all my family about Ancaster Primary School's victory. Nick Watson, Corinne Winter, Tom Prosser and I had triumphed.

When it was bedtime I got into bed and tried to get to sleep, but I couldn't. I mean, how are you meant to get to sleep after a day like that? So I learnt my script for the end of term play, another challenge!

Jacob Storey (10)
Ancaster CE Primary School, Grantham

A Day In The Life Of Daisy (Dog)

I whined in my basket, yawning. I heard footsteps coming down to feed me from upstairs. My kind owner, Lauren, came and fed me and my best friend. I always enjoy my breakfast of Chappie. I knew my next plan was to keep out of the way and play in the garden.

I ran and chased birds for an hour. I was worn out. I jumped and stretched on my white fleece on the dark green deckchair sunbathing.

My owner came out and found me sunbathing in the sun. I ran up to her. My best friend was on his lead. I then knew I was going for a walk. We got in the car and my owner's mum drove us up to the church. I knew that no one would be going to church on a Saturday. We jumped out of the car and walked over the road. At the traffic lights we turned left and walked for fifty yards and quickly crossed over and went down the woody path. After chasing squirrels and rabbits I slept for the rest of the day, dreaming of being a millionaire.

I soon woke when I heard my Bonios in my small blue colourful bowl. I was happy.

Lauren Cook (11)
Ancaster CE Primary School, Grantham

A Day In The Life Of Poodles (Dog)

I woke up on the second day of school and I ran to my master, well she is not my master but I will call her master. I went in her room. She wouldn't wake up, so I licked and barked. Finally she got up and let me run in the garden while she made my food but I had to have a disgusting tablet in my food.

When it was 8.30 I went for a walk, then they walked in a big house called school. My master's mum played ball with me until I went and met my master again. Then we went for a walk around the block and try to find some friends to play with. A girl from high school came to play with me, because she loves me.

Later and we are at home. I have a rest and calm down after my walk and play with my friends. While I rested, I dreamed of how and what I did on my walk. I could run in the garden chasing big birds, small birds and fat birds. When all the birds had flown away my master's brother came out and played football with me. Then we all went in to have tea and I went to sleep ready for tomorrow, another exciting day!

Heather Nugent (11)
Ancaster CE Primary School, Grantham

A DAY IN THE LIFE OF JIMBO (MY FERRET)

Dear diary,

Today I saw a medium-sized thing fly over my master's large cage. My master came to me and said to himself, 'I can't believe I hit the stone right over the house.' Then he took me out of my cage and let his brother hold me.

He was moving some stuff around. He took me back from his brother and put me down. I knew when he put me down that I had to go where the weird stuff was leading me.

Then my master said, 'He seems to like the obstacle course.' So I knew what it was. I did like the whatever course but after that I had to go back in my cage.

I started scratching on the cage door but nothing happened. Then I saw him coming out again and he gave me some food. I like chicken dog food best, but I do like a change though.

After I had my food, I went to sleep because I was tired. I dreamed I was in another obstacle course, it was a race and I won!

James Taylor (9)
Ancaster CE Primary School, Grantham

HORROR STORY

Our headmaster is Mr Smathe. His attitude to children wasn't very good at all. To him children were disgusting creatures that got things for him. The children at the school were treated like dirt and looked like something disgusting, like a dead animal. He had a short fuse and liked to take it out on children. It would be, 'Do this. Do that. Fetch me this. Fetch me that.' But his favourite was, 'Detention!'

The children were mysteriously disappearing. The rumour was that the teachers were eating them but that was ridiculous, or was it?

'Detention!' the dreaded sound of the teachers' call for food. Who was it? Who was going to be lunch for the teachers? Calum, my best friend, got up to be eaten. 'Let's make a run,' said the remaining children. We ran out of the classroom. The children were falling dead around me. I jumped out of the window and ran for my life. I ran and ran and ran until I reached a little hut where they could not find me.

Phillip Best (11)
Carr Lane Junior School, Willerby

WORLD WAR II

I led my squad out of the trenches and onto the battlefield. We marched forwards with our rifles in the air. As we stepped closer to Germany's territory, a gunshot pierced a man's throat on the left of me. But we carried on.

Eventually I told everybody to take aim and fire. The gunfire caused about five Germans to collapse on the ground. I ordered the sniper to lay down on the ground and take out the German commander. Suddenly loud cracks came from the German's base as three bullets came speeding through the sniper's forehead causing blood to go on my uniform.

I ordered a full attack towards the Germans. As we entered no-man's-land the man on the far right had his leg blown off by a mine. Two bullets sliced through the skin of my leg. I fell to the ground clutching my leg in agony. My whole life flashed before my eyes, including my wife and children. Two surgeons came with a stretcher.

I woke up in a hospital back in England to hear people celebrating that we had won the war against Germany. I was glad that I survived World War II.

Matthew Ives (10)
Carr Lane Junior School, Willerby

YOU'RE IN CHARGE

'Now, I'm just going out for a while and I'm leaving you in charge until I get back,' shouted Pete the boss.

Rob, who was left on his own, had to look after the library but decided to go on his lunch break instead, leaving nobody there at all.

Whilst Pete was out he was wondering what was going on in the library, and he was having second thoughts about whether he should have left Rob in charge.

After an hour Pete rushed back to the library and walked slowly down the aisle. He couldn't hear anything and he couldn't see anything. There was silence. Pete shouted, 'Rob, are you there?' There was no reply. Pete was feeling really bad now because he had left him in charge.

After ten minutes Rob came rushing into the library, thinking there was no one about, but then he heard someone cough.

Rob nervously walked down the aisle thinking who it was. Rob stopped thinking who it could be. Pete walked forwards. He stopped and shouted, 'Rob!'

Rob answered quietly as they walked towards each other. 'I wish I'd never left the library, I'm sorry.'

Sarah Whitham (11)
Carr Lane Junior School, Willerby

Not Just A Friend, An Even Better Friend

It all started when I was in Year 5, about two years ago. My friend, Rachel, just started school. She walked into the classroom about ten minutes after the bell rang with the headmaster.

She had long blonde hair, blue eyes and was tall.

During break we met and started talking. After school she invited me round to her house, although we had been friends for just a couple of hours.

Next day there was no school so me and Mum went out to town and bought a friendship bracelet for me and Rachel.

When I went back to school I went to my class and I gave her the bracelet. The headmaster then came and spoke to the teacher and the teacher said, 'Could Lauren please go to the headmaster's office?'

Rachel looked at me like I knew what this was about. The headmaster said, 'I understand you have been bullying Scott Padle.' Then there was a knock on the headmaster's door. 'Come in,' said the headmaster.

It was Rachel and she knew what it was about. She said, 'Lauren didn't do it. I did.'
'You may now leave Lauren.'

Rachel came out fifteen minutes later. I said thanks a lot to her and now we could be best friends.

Lauren Haley (11)
Carr Lane Junior School, Willerby

KIDNAPPED

The scream was louder than ever. He was coming to get me. But I don't understand . . . I don't belong to them. The only reason they have kidnapped me is because my mother has a diamond that her mother passed onto her when she died.

The kidnappers said, 'You can go home when we get that diamond but until then, you stay here.' Sherry is my kidnapper, but I don't tell them my name. All I tell them is that I want to go home.

After a few days I was ready to break free. I slowly opened my door and walked onto the mucky floor, still making sure they were in the shed. I ran out of the back door.

'Oi, get back!' shouted one of the nasty men. I stopped still with fear then ran as fast as I could.

About half an hour later I reached my street. My face lit up when I saw my house. I ran into the garden. Mum came out with her eyes filling up with tears. 'Mum, give them the diamond or they will take me again.'
'OK,' said Mum.

Then they pulled up in the car and snatched the diamond.
'Mum, what will Gran think?' I said.
'She will be proud we got you back.' said Mum.

Selesha Flanagan (10)
Carr Lane Junior School, Willerby

WHO AM I?

I never knew how hard it would be having the life of a super hero. It all started one day in a lab. I was taking photos of radioactive spiders when Mary Jane, my friend said, 'A spider's missing. There's supposed to be fifteen, but there's only fourteen. One has escaped!'

After a while she calmed down and I told her nothing bad would happen. But she started droning on about getting super spider powers but I had other things on my mind. The spider we were talking about was on my little finger and was crawling onto my hand. Then it bit me. I felt a quick rushing pain in my wrists. Then all I remember is waking up in my bed and some sort of web coming out of my wrists and sticking to my lamp.

The next day an old man said to me, 'You're changing kid and you'll be like me very soon!'
'Not exactly like you!' I said.

Later that night I noticed grip on my fingers. I tried climbing up my bedroom wall. I'm like a spider, I thought. The next day I made a red and blue suit. Who am I? I'm Spider-Man!

Sean Meek (11)
Carr Lane Junior School, Willerby

The Haunted Attic

One night, just after school had finished, a girl called Mandy and a boy called Andy couldn't wait to tell their story. That day they had overheard some teachers talking about something in the attic. They couldn't help thinking about what it was, so they went to investigate.

After everyone had gone home they both crept around school until they reached the attic. Before they opened the lid they heard footsteps coming down the hall. Andy said, 'Who could it be? All the teachers and children have gone home.'

They both stood behind the door and pushed it open slightly so they could see who it was. But then the footsteps stopped.

'They went into the classroom of 45,' Mandy said. 'Come on while we have the chance.'
They came out of the door and went to the attic. As they went up the stairs they saw lots of junk.

As they walked around Mandy spotted a box. It looked like a treasure box. It said on the top, *For teachers only*.
'Don't open it,' said Andy, 'it could be a spell.'

But she didn't listen. She opened it. Silence fell.

Abbie Kirk (10)
Carr Lane Junior School, Willerby

The Spider From Another Planet

I have never told this story until today about something that has ruined my life forever.

It all began one day at home in the countryside of Australia and my family were outside. My name's Jack Smith. I've got two brothers, a mum and a dad.

We were picking fruits from the garden, when my dad asked me to go into the forest and get some special flowers which can be made into food, so I got my equipment and took a stroll into the forest.

Usually there wasn't anything really dangerous. It took me three hours to get there and I was exhausted, but I was close and then there was the most mysterious bug that I had ever seen. It looked like a spider - part orange, part blue and part green.

I went up to it and it bit me. It just stung for a while and then it went off. I got the plants I wanted and ran home.

The next day I went up to the mirror and had a look at myself. Aarrgh! I looked horrible. I was green, blue and orange. I ran into the forest and I never saw my family ever again.

Daniel Thirkettle (11)
Carr Lane Junior School, Willerby

YOU'RE IN CHARGE

'I wish I had never done it,' shouted Lou.

Lou was a young little boy who lived with his family. It all started when his Mum left him in a room by himself and told him, 'You're in charge now. I'll just be a minute,' and then a horrid idea came over him.

Lou was in the living room. The TV was on and the fire was burning. 'Yeah,' Lou was swinging from the light on the ceiling. 'Aaah!' he shouted. *Bang!* Lou fell onto the settee and had gone right through it. Lou ripped up the carpet - *tear!* And played ball. *Smash!* went the ornaments on the fireplace. 'Argh, I scored,' roared Lou jumping up. Then he heard footsteps coming.

'Oh no!' whispered Lou. He had realised what he had done. The handle turned and the door creaked open.
'Argh!' screamed his mother. 'What have you done?'
The light and the shade were on the floor. The carpet was ripped up. The settee had a hole in it and the ornaments were in bits on the ground.
'I will never trust you again.'

Victoria Brown (11)
Carr Lane Junior School, Willerby

Miss Megeden Strikes Again

Suddenly Monkey Man heard shouting. Towns People was hanging from a skyscraper with loads of dynamite attached to him. He then saw Miss Megeden with a detonator in her hand.

Monkey Man knew he had to act quickly. He fired a banana string and swung from the roof of the hotel, where he was standing, to the skyscraper.

Miss Megeden was about to press the button on the detonator when Monkey Man shot it right out of her hand and it fell quickly to the floor.

But it was too late, Towns People was blown to pieces, even the skyscraper was blown up and thousands of people died. The question now was, did Monkey Man and Miss Megeden die too?

When the smoke cleared Monkey Man could be seen tied up. Miss Megeden had caught him and was going to kill him with a gun. She took him to her secret laboratory under the ground.

Then there was a bang, had Monkey Man been shot? No! Monkey Man had turned the gun on Miss Megeden, she had been shot in the head.

Monkey Man walked out of the cave and said, 'Don't worry, you're safe now.'

Dominic Young (11)
Carr Lane Junior School, Willerby

Harry Potter And The Goblet Of Fire

Harry and the dragon creature were facing each other eye to eye. Harry called his broom. He saw the broom next to him. He climbed on and flew off into the air. The dragon fired a fireball at him. Harry dodged it but only just. He charged straight at the dragon who swished its tail to try and hit him. But it . . . missed.

He cast a spell and the dragon turned into a frog. Then it just fell to the floor and crashed.

Harry found an egg, it had a note inside it. The note said 'You must find the Goblet of Fire'. So, Harry set off with some of his friends to find it.

An hour later Harry had found it and gathered his mates back together to tell them the story.

James Milestone (11)
Carr Lane Junior School, Willerby

CHANGES

Louise's mum was helping her to pack her bags to stay at her dad's for a while. Louise had never seen her dad since he left when she was just three years old. Louise is thirteen now and it was from today that there would be some changes.

'Hurry up Mum,' shouted Louise from the taxi. 'We are going to be late.

Finally they arrived at her dad's house after two boring hours in a boiling hot taxi. 'Does my dad really own this massive place?' said Louise to her mum.
'Yeap. Well come on, we can't keep your dad waiting.'

Louise and her mum went in. For the first time in ten years she saw her dad and there was a girl that looked just like her standing next to him. It was as if she were looking in a mirror. Her mum and dad told Louise and Katie they were twin sisters and that their mum and dad were getting back together again.

Rachel Key (11)
Carr Lane Junior School, Willerby

YOU'RE IN CHARGE

I couldn't believe what I had just done. How was I going to tell my father?

It all started with my father leaving me in charge of the hotel. Everything was going smoothly at first, and I had only gone upstairs for a few minutes. When I came back there was a bunch of unhappy customers.

As I was pretty inexperienced, I didn't really know how to handle them. I nervously trembled towards the desk and asked them what was wrong. 'We could not get out toilet to flush and when it did it flooded the entire bathroom. And when we tried to get away from all the hassle at the swimming pool, we found it was closed, when it said *'Open 24 hours, 7 days a week!'* yelled one of the unhappy customers.

Suddenly my blood started to boil. 'Right, I've had enough of all you people complaining when nothing's wrong. Get out, all of you!' I bellowed.
'With pleasure,' they ignorantly replied.

Just as they hurried out my dad waddled in. How could I tell him? I would never be trusted again.

Andrew Hancocks (10)
Carr Lane Junior School, Willerby

Best Friends And Dreams

'See you all next week,' shouted Mr Burns over the screeching noise of chairs, 'and don't forget to hand in your homework unless you want a detention that is,' he added.
'Wait for me,' shouted Kelly.
'Well hurry up then,' answered Gemma sarcastically.

Kelly and Gemma had been the best of friends for over five years and they always stuck together. Although they liked school, they hated chemistry class and were always glad when it finished. The two girls walked up to the school gate and said their goodbyes.

A few hours later Kelly had a text message from Gemma asking if she would like to hang out in the park. She replied yes and set off. When she arrived, Gemma was waiting for her on the swings. Kelly sat down beside her and they began to talk.

'Have you seen that magazine with the interview with Leonardo di Caprio?' asked Kelly excitedly.
'Yes, I wish I could go and meet him,' replied Gemma.
'Me too,' added Kelly.

On and on they talked until it began to get dark. 'We'd better get going,' said Kelly miserably.
'See you tomorrow,' replied Gemma.

Saturday finally came and it was time to take their horses out for a ride. They mounted on top of them and rode off. As they trotted on the road they noticed a leaflet asking for talent. 'Look!' shouted Gemma. 'Wow, let's sign up.'

They signed up and carried on. As for the rest of the story, well what do you think?

Rebecca Gilson (10)
Carr Lane Junior School, Willerby

THE NOISE

One day Stacey set off on a walk through the wood to get to her friend's house. Stacey was in the middle of the forest when she heard a terrifying noise. It gave her pimples all over and her body hairs were sticking up on her back.

It stopped and then started again. She spun around and around looking for where it was coming from. She carried on spinning. 'Stop it!' she screamed. She started running in the opposite direction. She ran but all she could hear was the noise that she couldn't describe. She ended up on the floor of the wood, screaming and shouting.

A few days later a man on his horse heard the screaming and saw Stacey crying herself to sleep. He got off his horse and picked the girl up so she could stand. The man, horrified, backed away from the girl. He backed and backed away further when he saw her eyes rolling up and down. As he backed she grabbed the man and chucked him against the tree. He fell on the ground. She thought he was still on the floor, but he surprised her by banging her head with a log.

Some people think it killed her but others think she's out there.

Raine Partis (11)
Carr Lane Junior School, Willerby

ONE UNFORGETTABLE DAY

'Oh yes!' I yelled. My dad had won a holiday in a mystery destination.
'When are we going Mum?' I politely asked.
'Well, it says the 23rd of May, 2002. That's *tomorrow!* We'd better get packing,' panicked Mum.

A couple of hours later we were ready to go. Everything was perfect and we could finally get some sleep.

We woke early the next morning. Annie, my sister, was in a ratty mood as usual. We loaded up the car and left for the airport. It was a long trip but we got there and got straight on the plane.

After two and a half hours we arrived. It was extremely dark and there was a howling in the distance that sent a chill up my spine. Soon after we got to the apartment. It was falling apart and it was even worse inside. Bloodstained carpets covered the rotten floorboards.

That night was sleepless and the next morning there were chairs and tables floating, smashed cutlery all through the house and animal tracks imprinted on the floor.
'I've seen enough, this is outrageous! I'm leaving this instance,' screamed Mum.
'Me too!' boomed Dad in an angry tone.

We packed our bags, left and were never seen again. Some say we got on a plane and left, others say we got eaten alive by werewolves but only we know the truth.

Ryan Hall (10)
Carr Lane Junior School, Willerby

RALLY DISASTER

It was the 22nd of June and it was the English rally. There was a new driver, David Skelton. He had joined the Peugeot team. David and his co-driver had done really well in the first stage and were hoping to do just as well in the second.

They were setting off in seventh place - that was a good position. Sixth had gone and David was ready to go. He whipped his car up to second and sped off. Right, left, right, left. He sped thorough the muddy maze of trees and bushes.

He was climbing up a very steep hill with a tight left at the top. There was another steep hill coming with a very, very tight right at the top. David sped up the hill and forgot about the corner and sped off the track. They started to fall 9,000 feet to a frozen lake at the bottom.

Crack! They hit the bottom. A spectator called for an ambulance and they both were rushed to hospital. Dave woke up very weak. He realised he was in hospital. He asked the nurse to call Mandy, his girlfriend, so she could come and see him. He asked the nurse how his co-driver was. 'Better than you,' the nurse said.

Mandy arrived and as she was coming through the door Dave had a fit and died. 'No!' Mandy yelled.

Joseph Cooper (11)
Carr Lane Junior School, Willerby

HAUNTED!

I opened the door of the house and walked in. It was dark apart from a few dimly lit candles in floating cages. But the thing that got me all goose pimply was a floating cart track which spiralled into the air, with cart after cart of potions whizzing around and around.

I thought I would be able to get out if I could just get there. 'Ah ha!' I said. There was a high sloped staircase which led near the track, so all I had to do was jump from the banister.

I cautiously walked up the staircase and felt it move. I was right, it swung me 90 degrees and left me on a platform near to the track. Then I saw a cart coming. It was full of bats' wings but it would do, so I braced myself and jumped onto the cart.

It took about half an hour before I saw something amazing. Two hands were loading potions into trolleys then I saw a hand fall. It fell down and down and looked as if it fell into a black hole. I shouted for help.

Suddenly the cart swung into fast mode and stopped outside a door. It would have to do, I jumped out and pulled on the door. I looked down and saw the black hole was getting higher and wider. It was sucking stuff in. I crossed my fingers and hoped.

David Skelton (11)
Carr Lane Junior School, Willerby

ESCAPED FROM DEATH!

One summer holiday Chloe and her friend Terry were playing with Terry's toy plane. It was Chloe's turn to throw the plane and she threw it a long, long way. It went so far that they couldn't find it. They looked absolutely everywhere and they still couldn't find it. Then they looked up the hill near where they were playing. At the top was a creepy old farmhouse.

They headed towards the house. They were both terrified of what was in there. When they got to the house they knocked on the dusty, old wooden door. The door slowly creaked open. They cautiously went in and had a look around. Then they heard a sound - a very scary sound. Since Chloe was the bravest, she went first to see what it was. It turned out to be a big, hairy wolf.

Chloe and Terry ran the fastest they'd ever run. Then they heard a life saving screaming saying, 'Noo!'

When they looked down, they realised they were just about to run over the edge of a steep cliff that would have killed them if they had not stopped. They're lucky to be alive.

Jayne Witherwick (11)
Carr Lane Junior School, Willerby

TEN KINGDOMS

Hi, I'm Emma and this is my story of the 10th kingdom.

It starts off when I'm about to leave work and I go through the woods. I usually go through there because that's where I left my best friend, Wolf. Wolf is a good guy, but when a full moon comes he has the instincts of a wolf.

'Hello Emma, it's me Wolf!'
'Hi Wolf, what are you doing here?'
'You have to come to the other kingdoms because your mum has become queen and has taken Prince Bob into hostage.'

So, here we are in the other kingdoms and Wolf feels hungry. We go past a field of sheep and then I realise that I'm in Sheep Town and a full moon is about to happen and that's when he gets his wolf instincts.

'Come on Wolf, it's time to find a place to stay because we're now about 900 miles away.'
'That's not far,' said Wolf excitedly.

As we went through Sheep Town, we found a place to stay which was called Baa Hotel. The next day Wolf was covered in blood, there was only one explanation. 'Wolf, your instincts have started!'
Wolf ran all the way to Bubble Town. Luckily I managed to keep up.

Finally we made it to the palace. 'Mum, Mum, where are you? Mum, please come out!'
'Looking for me child,' she said.

I grabbed the closest sharp object near me and stabbed it through her heart. 'Ahhh!'

Suddenly I woke up, it was only a dream.

Nicky Rudd (11)
Carr Lane Junior School, Willerby

If Birds Could Fly I Can!

My name is Tom but people call me Tich. I'm not around now but just this once I will tell you the spookiest story ever.

When I was on Earth I wanted to fly like mad, so of course, I wanted to be an inventor.

One day, one sunny day, I was walking down a street thinking about my inventions, and I thought, I will even make a deal with the Devil if people could fly. Then this guy jumped me. He had red, glaring eyes and said, 'You wish that you could fly. Well I could give you whatever you want if you go into me,' with his dark sneering voice.
'Never!' I shouted and with a scream of smoke he had gone.

I was very old (31 to be exact) when I finally had a breakthrough. I invented the smartest technology that ever lived. I invented a flying machine so I decided to try it out. I did and it worked. I went higher and higher. I could not stop. I could not breathe. This evil laugh followed me.

Nobody knows what happened to me. People now fly everywhere but I was the first man to try it.

Stacey Roche (11)
Carr Lane Junior School, Willerby

The Werewolf Rock Band

Once on a dark night, in a dark forest, in a haunted house, four young men walked through a transforming machine with four wolves and their DNA mixed and it formed four werewolves. They soon became a good band together and called themselves the Werewolf Rock Band.

One night they had their first concert. They got their guitar, drums, the deck and the microphone. Rampage Ryan was the singer, Mental Matty was the guitar player, Jiggy with it Jack was on the drums and Punk Hair Paul was the DJ. The first concert was nearly over. Just then a boy climbed up on stage. 'Let's do this,' whispered Matty.
'Yes, let's show this clown who he's dealing with,' replied Ryan.

Matty pulled the third string from the right and a huge knife popped out the end of his guitar. Ryan pressed a button on his microphone and a small dagger poked out of the top of it. Jack twisted a drumstick and a small knife sprung out of the top of it and Paul picked up a sharpened disc and all at once, stab, stab, stab, chop.

The boy fell from the stage as still as ice, then everything went silent. The police came and took the band to the station and told them their music career was over.

Jack Reger (11)
Carr Lane Junior School, Willerby

The Malca Effect

One year ago on a planet called Racata there lived a girl, Zarlar. She lived with her mum in an apartment which was just near her mum's work. Her mum worked for a company that specialised in Earthling stuff.

One day Zarlar's mum was informed that she had to go to Earth and find a substance called Malca. 'How long will you be away for?' Zarlar asked.
'Well Zarlar, you can come with me but I'm not sure how long we'll be gone,' she replied.

The flight to Earth was very long, as they had to travel through three galaxies.

Once on the planet, the crew had a job finding a spot to set up camp. They went through trees after trees after trees until they finally found a spot to camp. Zarlar, although happy that she could now rest, felt something wrong - danger was around.

The next day Zarlar and the rest of the crew set off to search for the Malca. When suddenly Zarlar and her mum found themselves alone.
'Where's everyone gone?' Zarlar asked.
'I don't know,' stuttered her mum.

It took a long time before Zarlar and her mum found camp. However, they had a big surprise when they got back. All the crew were on the floor and not moving. 'Why are they on the floor?' asked Zarlar.

Her mum rushed over to a man who seemed to be waking up from a deep sleep. He said, 'It's . . . the Malca . . . don't drink . . . big sleep.'

But (not understanding what he said) she drank the Malca and fell straight to sleep.

Zarlar knew she should feel worried and she did but she couldn't help remembering a story she was told by her dad, where a princess fell into a deep sleep and was woken by a prince's kiss. Then it clicked. She first went to her mum and kissed her on the forehead; her mum, surprisingly, woke up instantly.

After ages of just kissing; the crew, plus Zarlar and her mum went back home.

Two weeks after Zarlar was awarded with a medal.

Lucy Henderson (11)
Carr Lane Junior School, Willerby

MYRETRIONS

Crash! Bang! Wollop! 'What as that?' murmured Gally.

Dad was speechless. Dad ran back upstairs and shouted, 'Get out of the house everybody!'
'Why?' cried Mum.
'Because there is a big merchant spaceship outside in our backyard,' said Dad. My heart rate was beating 5005 times per two minutes.

'Ahhh!' shouted everyone in the house, 'It's a merchant spaceship. Ah!'
'Shut up,' shouted Dad, 'I'll go out and fight the aliens with a chainsaw and spade.'

I looked outside, they were hideous creatures, they stank of cow muck and their bodies were as ugly as a two-headed mongrel. Their teeth stuck out with sharp points on the end and saliva dripped out of the gigantic holes in their heads.

Mum and Gally looked out of the window and saw Dad with a load of blood dripping down his body and massive rips in his tank top. 'Dad, are you all right?' said Gally.
'Yeah, I am doing all right,' said Dad.
'Gally come on, do what you father told you to do.'

Gally had one more look and saw Dad lying on the floor whilst the aliens were taking off. They ran outside and looked at Dad to see if he was dead, but he had survived.

Matthew Chester (11)
Carr Lane Junior School, Willerby

What Was That?

Thump! Crash! What was that? I looked at my alarm clock as I sat up. It was the middle of the night and I was always waking up - even if I heard the faintest of noises. But this noise was louder.

I climbed out of my warm, *safe* bed and put my slippers on. I stood up and tiptoed towards the stairs, terrified of what I might find at the bottom. I walked down hearing more crashes. My heart was thumping like a drum.

When I finally got to the bottom I crept into the tiny room silently. I found it was a complete mess - vases knocked over, curtains pulled down and chairs disturbed. I was shocked at what the burglars (or so I thought) had done.

I was just about to turn around to go to my mum when I heard a noise, a howling noise. It sounded like a ghost. Maybe it was! I froze in what seemed like a fantasy world with ghosts and witches. Something soft brushed past my leg. I looked down and saw my cat staring up at me. Then I realised something. How could the burglar have got in? There were no windows smashed and everything was locked. It must have been my cat all along.

Rachel Kendall (11)
Carr Lane Junior School, Willerby

GHOST AT NUMBER 13!

Everyone thought there was a ghost at 13 Oak Street, but there wasn't any proof so I went to investigate. My name is Harry Simpson and I am not frightened of anything.

Later I searched the house for a whole hour and I found nothing but bats and spiders. 'Now I will be able to prove there are no ghosts,' I said.

Suddenly a white figure rose out of the darkness of the room. Then I realised in front of me was a *ghost!* I froze and the room froze with me. *'Help!'* I screamed. I sped towards the door and fiddled with the handle. *'Locked!'* I squealed. I was stuck with a 1,000-year-old ghost.

'Come,' the ghost whispered. He grabbed my shoulder. I turned as white as snow. 'Come,' the ghost repeated.
He took me down endless flights into a dark, misty room. He lit a candle. I could see now. We were in a stone-walled room of a *torture chamber. 'Help!'* I shouted.

So now I am here. The ghost has gone but that is the least of my worries because at the moment I am hanging over a pool of alligators and if I move my legs I will *fall!*

Victoria Hussey (11)
Carr Lane Junior School, Willerby

Blast-Off

My name is George James Lucas. I am going to tell you a very weird and mysterious story, so keep your ears open and listen, OK?

I really, really, really hate my stepsister, Sally. She is eleven years old, the same age as me as a matter of fact. It all started when me, Mum, my stepdad and my stepsister all went to the NASA Space Station to watch the launch of Apollo 13.

When we got into the control room, Sally suddenly burst out. I looked around and saw her on her hands and knees being sick. My stepdad, Andy, hurried off with Sally. She was holding a plastic bag in her hands.

'Come on,' said Mum, 'you should stay in here.' She opened a green door and left.
I walked over to it and sat down on a chair, then I turned a little blue television on . . . zzzz, bang. A picture of a launch pad came into view. Then numbers appeared at the top right hand corner of the screen and it read 10 to 0. Then a flash from Apollo's engine came, the rocket lifted out of sight.

But suddenly the rocket came down as fast as a bullet and *crash!*

Jamie Young (11)
Carr Lane Junior School, Willerby

Special Guest

'Mum, I am going to school now.'
'You'll be early, wait for another ten minutes.'
'No, I have to meet Sarah at the bus stop.'
'Why?'
'Because a special guest is coming so we want to get there early to see her first.'
'Go on then Claire, but be back by four because your . . .' *Slam!* 'tea will be ready.'

Claire ran as fast as she could go. There was Sarah waiting for Claire at the bus stop. 'Hi Sarah.'
'Hi Claire. Here's the bus.'

Claire and Sarah got on the old bus. 'Look, there's a limo and it's heading towards our school!'
'Maybe it's our special guest. I wonder who it is. Don't you?'
'Yes.'

Ten minutes passed and they arrived at school. But they were ten minutes early anyway, but there were lots of children on the playground.

After an hour the special guest went to see the head teacher. Five minutes later they could hear her shoes coming down the corridor. Claire had butterflies in her tummy. The door opened slowly. There she was, Holly Valance.

Lucy Baker (11)
Carr Lane Junior School, Willerby

SAM'S HORRIBLE NIGHT

What was that? That sound, didn't you hear it? he thought to himself. Sam got out of bed and slowly walked down the creaky staircase. 'I . . . is anyone there?'

Sam heard the sound again and again. He crept into the kitchen, his hand shaking like a leaf. He reached for the light switch. 'I will ring the police in a minute if you don't show yourself,' he said.
There wasn't any one in there but he could still hear that sound. He picked up telephone and started to dial 999.
'Hello, how can I help you?'
'The police please.'
'Where to?'
'79 Wellwood Street.'
'OK. They will be there in a second.'

A second later - *knock, knock.* 'Come in.'

They went upstairs first and then down but they didn't find anything.

In the end it was only Hammey, Sam's hamster. 'Hammey, what were you doing? You made me scared. I thought someone was in the house. I think tomorrow we will have to buy a new hamster ball because that one is too squeaky.'

It was now 1 o'clock in the morning and Sam was getting really tired so he went back up the creaky staircase and back into bed. He was nearly asleep and then he heard the sound again.

Hannah Cooper (11)
Carr Lane Junior School, Willerby

Don't Turn The Light On

There were two women and they had been best friends since year 3. They got nicknamed 'The Perfectionists' but their real names were Nicki Kellaway and Maria Marison.

One dark, rainy night Nicki decided to go clubbing, leaving Maria alone in a bad area. Nicki got a taxi and left.

When she got there she realised she had left her bag with her money in at the house, so she frantically went home. She opened the door, not bothering to turn the light on, and grabbed her bag then left.

The next morning Nicki was on her way home, as she'd been clubbing all night. She opened the door to find Maria dead, then she saw the message written in blood on the wall saying *'I bet you're glad you didn't turn the light on'*.

Nicki then froze, she called 999 and told them what had happened. They never found the killer. He's probably still lurking around out there now.

Emily Petch (11)
Carr Lane Junior School, Willerby

A Weird Scary Tale

One scary night in the dark, dark freaky graveyard, I was walking along. Suddenly it felt like someone was following me, but no one was there. I heard something, zombies!

'Arghh!' I ran as fast as a cheetah to find something to hide behind. Wherever I went, they went. I didn't know what the heck was going on. One of them started singing. He looked a bit like Michael Jackson, but then he got his knife out - he didn't try to stab me though.

They suddenly took their masks off and said, 'You're in a Michael Jackson scene.' I was very confused then they started laughing more. 'We're joking. We're your best friends. We've got you back for squirting us last week with your humungous super soaker!'

Scott Annandale (11)
Carr Lane Junior School, Willerby

THE GREEN CAR

This story is from a friend of a friend of mine.

It was a full moon and Lucy and James were going down an old road in their red Rover. Suddenly a green car came out of nowhere. Lucy looked in her back mirror and there was no one driving. They pulled up and got out of the car and the car had gone, and all that was left were tyre marks.

When they got back in the car James saw the green car behind them again. They decided to speed up a bit, passing the speed limit. As soon as they entered the main road, they realised they had gotten a fine for speeding. They tried to explain about the green car but it had disappeared.

Lucy and James started to try and find some information about the old road. According to the library there used to be a car factory which sold green cars and every year they had a competition. Bill Sad won, but his friend was mean and murdered him. Bill Sad now haunted the old country road. We had seen a ghost!

Imogen Mercer Swain (11)
Carr Lane Junior School, Willerby

AMERICAN WEREWOLF IN VENICE

'We're gonna miss the plane.' Jake, Bryan and John were flying to the streets of Venice. As they got onto the plane, there was a very strange figure sitting at the front near the cockpit.

When they got to the Italian airport there was a butler waiting for their arrival. He picked up their bags and murmured, 'Come along please.' They were escorted to a nearby mansion.

It was a full moon. Jake stared into the bushes. It started shaking, shaking like a guinea pig. Suddenly a roaring creature pounced out and shredded part of Jake's skin off, blood was pouring out. Jake fainted . . .

Next morning Jake woke up thinking it was all a terrible nightmare. Then he felt a large pain in his ankle. He glared, his heart pounded.

John called room service not knowing Jake had half his leg off. Jake thought about the saying, the werewolf that turns you, you need to eat its heart to turn to human again.

As they strolled to the Italian restaurant they saw the same person from the plane. They started shaking him. That very same night he turned into a werewolf. Jake pounced out ripping its heart out and eating it.

Nick Johnson (11)
Carr Lane Junior School, Willerby

The Haunted School

One very dark night after school, Andy had a sleep over at his house. Everyone was talking about the school, saying that it was haunted because of all the noises you can hear at lunch time.

The next day, when Andy got to school, he started his first lesson. While he was working he heard a noise, a cold and screechy chill. After school I want to find out what is really happening in here, Andy thought to himself.

That night Andy snuck out of his window and crept into the school playground. He could see white lights coming from inside the school, then he saw a figure in the darkness. When he got closer he saw something move. Andy crept into the school and a load of ghosts flew after him and chased him home.

That night he promised himself he wouldn't go to school at night again.

Mark Cressey (11)
Carr Lane Junior School, Willerby

The Tournament

Who is the true legend?

There is a tournament of martial arts and twenty people are fighting for the trophy. The two people who are the main threat are Jackie Chan and Bruce Lee.

The tournament is held at Smash Castle and the first match is between Jackie Chan and Ogamicthtue. It is a duel to the death. They bow to each other and the fight begins.

Jackie Chan flips in the air and does a flying kick, but the other guy does ten punches to his face. Jackie Chan is really angry and flies into the air. He breaks the guy's neck by punching him right in his lungs and kills him. Jackie Chan has loads of blood on his hand.

All of the other fights go by and the last match is between Jackie Chan and Bruce Lee.

The match goes on for two hours and the ending of it is when Bruce Lee kills Jackie Chan with a kick that goes right through his body. It kills him instantly, so Bruce Lee wins the tournament and gets the trophy.

Alex Edge (10)
Carr Lane Junior School, Willerby

THE HAUNTING

It was a Saturday morning, Matt and Joe had just had breakfast and were packing for an adventure that they would never forget. As they set off Joe kept thinking that they had forgotten something. They had forgotten their torch.

As they walked up the lane the forest came into view. The forest was about ten miles by eight miles long. It was one of the biggest forests in the world.

As they got deeper into the forest, they found a perfect resting spot to eat their dinner. When Matt looked at his watch it was four o'clock, so Joe said, 'I think we should go.' So they set off down the road and back home.

'Matt, it's this way isn't it?'
'Yes, I think so.'
'OK, then let's go.'

About two hours later they stopped. They were lost and they didn't know what to do, and it was getting dark. One hour later it was pitch-black. 'I can't believe you forgot to pack torches.'
'I told you I was sorry.'

Suddenly there was a loud howl, so they ran and ran until the noise stopped. Then they could hear rustling. 'It could be them.'
'Just be quiet and go to sleep,' and they both fell asleep under the shelter of a bush.

That night all the animals came out and kept guard over their two human visitors. Matt and Joe were none the wiser as they slept through the whole thing.

Callum Williams (11)
Carr Lane Junior School, Willerby

The Look-A-Like

Looking like a celebrity isn't all that good. I mean, it was good at first but now it's just annoying. I walk down the street and I hear, 'Can I have your autograph please, Britney Spears?' Gee, that is so annoying. For *heaven's sake*, I am not Britney!

I was taking my usual walk down the road to the ice cream parlour. There was this man in a black car and a black suit, he watched me walk in. His eyes were like an owl's. He followed me. This girl asked me for my autograph. I said, 'I am not Britney.'
'Please Britney, it's for my daughter, she is in hospital. Please?'
'OK then I will, who's got a pen?'

The guy that followed me in gave me his pen. I signed and the guy left without his pen. I chased after him and said, 'You've forgotten your pen,'
He turned round and said, 'Britney Spears, you have the right to remain silent, but anything you do say may be given in evidence when you later rely on it in court.'
'But . . . but . . . I haven't done anything.'
'Not paying your taxes for ten years. I think that's a crime.'
'Nooo! I'm not Britney Spears.'

The policeman did not believe me as he'd watched me sign her name.

Dawn Gray (11)
Carr Lane Junior School, Willerby

SPORTS DAY

'Mum, are you coming to our sports day?'
'Might do, see how I'm feeling,' answered Mum.
'Well, we've been practising all week at school Mum.'

Danny is talking to his mum trying to persuade her to come to his sports day in a week. He keeps telling her that he is the best in the school at javelin.

'Just going to the shop, won't be long.'

Danny is thinking of what he can do. Ah, I'll go for a jog around the big block for practise. Right, where are my trainers? There they are.

Slam! That was the door. A few seconds later he had forgot a drink. *Slam!* That was the door again.

'Danny, where are you going?' shouted Danny's mum.
'For a jog around the big block. I've got a drink,' replied Danny, as he was at the edge of the street panting a little.

Danny's mum was thinking of cooking Danny's favourite tea because she thought he had behaved well.

Danny arrived home. 'Ah, that was good apart from it being tiring.'
'Danny, why don't you go get changed because you will be sweaty and smelly?' said Mum. 'Your tea will be ready when you come down.'
'OK,' said Danny.

While walking upstairs Danny knew his mum would go to sports day. Later on he was proven right.

Josh Simpson (11)
Crowle County Primary School, Nr Scunthorpe

A One Day Nightmare

'Aagghh!' I screamed. 'What's going on?' In the mirror I didn't see myself, but what I could see was Alice, and I was in her house and in her body.
'Come on Alice, we've got to be at school,' called Tia (Alice's older sister.) I couldn't believe what was happening. She must be in my body - Alice in my body, oh no!

At school it was terrible. Alice (though everyone thinks she's Tess) started shouting out loud. 'I fancy Declan.' Tomorrow if I'm back in my body it's going to be my worst nightmare because Declan is ugly, thick, smelly and scruffy. She was even kissing him. Oh great, I thought, but what could I do to stop her? Tomorrow I'm going to die. All through lunch it was as bad as ever. At play I decided not to go out and see what was happening.

I walked home by myself, though the worst thing was that I had to go home to Alice's house instead of my own normal home. Tia walked into the kitchen. 'How did school go Alice, any good?'
Tia seems happy, I thought.
'Oh, it was okay,' I replied gloomily.

I went to bed at night-time hoping to be me again. The next day I looked into the mirror and found . . .

Kirsty Bowles (11)
Crowle County Primary School, Nr Scunthorpe

Dream World

I woke up one morning with the sun blazing in my window. I got dressed and went downstairs but when I got there no one was there. Usually there was always Mum there.

I went back upstairs and when I got there, it had all changed. My bedroom was not there, only a big puddle of water. Then I noticed I wasn't in the same place but a dream world full of all different things that I like. I went running round the place and then I went to a different area. Like my nightmare, it was full of all of my worst things, but I didn't care.

Suddenly I did care because there was something scary right in front of me. I ran as fast as I could but it still kept up with me. Then I noticed an exit, I kept on running though.

Then I arrived in another place. This was worse though. I thought it could not get any worse but it could. Oh, much worse. It started to thunder with a bang. I tried to find shelter but there was none. Then I woke up, it was just a dream.

Sophie Colebrook (11)
Crowle County Primary School, Nr Scunthorpe

A Ghastly Ghostly Tale

A boy called Joe was walking in the woods when he noticed a big house covered with ivy. He tiptoed through the door to find bowls of cobwebbed covered candy on a table with a spider on. He walked towards the table and fell down a trapdoor.

Bang! He landed on a coffin and was flung off. A pale man with black hair and sharp teeth sat up out of the coffin. 'Arrgh!' cowered Joe. 'You're a vampire.'
'Don't worry, you're safe, I'm friendly.'

Scratch, scratch. A white see-through ghost came dragging rusty chains. Joe stepped back and the wall collapsed. Out came a bear as big as a mountain snapping his jaw. Joe saw a door and ran to it. It closed and an overgrown gerbil scuttled down to Joe's feet. Neigh! Joe heard a horse being ridden by a headless horseman. Joe ran through the door to find the Devil bowling with a skeleton, using his skull as a ball and spikes for pins.

Joe ran through the door passing the vampire, ghost, bear, gerbil, headless horseman, Devil and skeleton and out. They all shouted, 'Come back, we only wanted a pizza!'

Kit Rawlings (11)
Crowle County Primary School, Nr Scunthorpe

THE REFLECTION IN THE POND

There once was a little girl. She was six. She loved to play in the garden by the pond. Her name was Lilly because she loved to watch the lily pads float across the pond when she was small.

Now she sits by the pond and drinks tea with her doll Ella. She loves to be in the garden because it is so beautiful with flowers all over the place, big oaks for shade and lush green grass. It is such a lovely place to be.

But sometimes she got lonely. She had Ella, but she wanted someone to play with. Lilly looked in the pond. She saw a girl in her reflection.
'Hello,' said the reflection.
'Who are you?' said Lilly.
'I'm your reflection. Can I play with you?' said the reflection.
'Oh, oh yes of course. I'm lonely, I have no one to play with,' moped Lilly.

So they played round the pond all day long. They played every day all the time. All of a sudden it started to rain, it went dull. Lilly's reflection disappeared. Lilly went in. Lilly and her reflection were best friends and played all the time except on dull days.

Samantha Stephens (11)
Crowle County Primary School, Nr Scunthorpe

A Trip To Old Trafford

It was the big day. Alex was getting ready for the big day. It was Man Utd against Leeds Utd. 'Hurry up, we'll be late,' Alex said.

It takes one and a half hours to get to Manchester. Alex has one brother, he's a big Man Utd fan, as well as Alex. They were both in their Man Utd reversible kits. They got into their Rover and their dad started to drive.

They got there thirty minutes early so they went to get something to eat, then they saw Man Utd players training so the got their autographs. Then the Leeds players came out to train so they booed them.

Then it was kick-off. The captains shook hands. Then the referee blew his whistle. The commentators were above us so we listened to them talking. Man Utd were on the attack and they passed it to Van Nistelrooy who blasted it into the net. The referee blew his whistle for half-time. Man Utd were leading by 1 goal to 0.

The second half wasn't any different. Man Utd were passing the ball around and just strolling. It was full-time. On the way home I fell asleep because I was tired.

Graeme Fletcher (10)
Crowle County Primary School, Nr Scunthorpe

CAMP!

Sarah and Jo were going on a camping trip with their school. It was Monday morning and Sarah and Jo were getting on the bus. 'I can't wait till we get to Camp Sunset. It's going to be so fun.'

'Yes, here at last. Let's go and find our tents. Come on everyone, let's go to bed.'

'Sarah, Sarah, did you hear that noise?' said Jo.
'Don't be silly Jo, it's nothing. It's just the wind,' said Sarah.
'But it sounds like a ghost. And it's coming from the woods.'
'Well let's go and investigate.'
'But I don't like going in the woods at night.'
'Don't be silly.'

Bang!

'Argh! What was that?'
'It's coming from over there. It's coming from tent 14.'
'Well let's go and see what it is.'
'But . . . but it's a ghost, run!'

'Miss, Miss, there's a ghost in tent 14.'
'Don't be silly girls. There's no such thing as ghosts.'
'But there is, look it's there.'
'Argh! Got you!'
'It's only Sam and Chloe messing about. Ha ha, that's not funny.'
'Night girls.'

'Come on girls, get your stuff packed. It's time to get on the bus.'

'I'm never going to Camp Sunset again!'

Chloe Stuart (11)
Crowle County Primary School, Nr Scunthorpe

A Day In The Life Of Emma Kitching

Emma woke up on Saturday morning. She went down to breakfast and went back up to get dressed. It was quarter to ten. Emma had to be at netball for ten o'clock. Mum shouted, 'Hurry up Emma.' Emma ran down the stairs and got in the car. Mum turned on the engine and set off to Epworth.

When Emma got to netball she paid money and went on the court. The teacher said, 'Everyone come get a ball and practise shooting.' Emma went to the far net and started trying to shoot. Emma shot three out of ten. The teacher said, 'Come back in.' She asked, 'How many did you shoot?' People put their hands up when it was the number that they shot. Then the teacher split the teams into four groups so they could practise playing against a team. When they had played every team, they sat on the court and the teacher chose a player of the week. Then it was half-past 12.

Emma's mum came to pick Emma up and take her home for lunch. Emma got in the car and went home. There were sandwiches on the table. After lunch Emma went out to play with her sister, Sarah. When she came back in tea was on the table. Emma ate her tea then she went for a bath, watched some TV until 9.00pm and then went to bed.

Sarah Kitching (11)
Crowle County Primary School, Nr Scunthorpe

THE TITANIC, THE SINKABLE SHIP

The year is 1912, the year of the Titanic. This is a real tale about the man who sunk the Titanic (well he claims it to be true). It started at the docks where the Titanic was. Everybody was flooding on. It seemed like the whole of England was there.

Our man was on-board. He was a weirdo. He was willing to put an end to his life and others. However, one thing stood in his way, how was he going to sink the ship? It was too big to sink, well on his own anyway, so he decided to get some help from the inside. 'I need some help to go and get some luggage,' said our man, Jim.
'OK Sir,' said the servant.

The servant followed Jim. As they went to the luggage room, he saw the guards. 'Good day Sir,' they said to Jim.
'I am looking for a Mr Jacobs and his luggage. Is he on guard?'

Then suddenly there was an explosion. The place was flooding. 'Water, water everywhere,' cried Jim.
'Sir!' cried the guard.

Glub! Glub! No one was to survive.

It sunk!

John Robinson (11)
Crowle County Primary School, Nr Scunthorpe

The Unidentified Planet

A long time ago there lived a boy called Owen whose ambition was to go into space. One day he was playing aliens in the garden and all of a sudden he shot up off the ground. He flew as fast as lightning and suddenly it went black.

When he awoke he was on a bed with bright lights dazzling him. Suddenly a dark figure appeared. 'Who are you?' Owen asked nervously.
'I'm called Blobble,' a voice replied.
'Please let me go!' Owen said scarcely.
'OK if you insist,' Blobble said.

Blobble lifted Owen off the bed and took him outside. 'This is the planet Anitneg,' Blobble explained. 'Let's eat.'

Owen and Blobble went into a snack bar where everyone was talking in a different language. 'What do you want?' Blobble asked.
'I don't know. Anything,' Owen said.
'OK, I'll get them,' Blobble said.

He walked up to the desk. 'I'll have two slobots on table four,' Blobble said. Then as if by magic the food appeared on the table. It was slugs' heads. 'How do I get home?' Owen asked.
'You can't,' Blobble said.

Will Owen get off the planet?

Lewis Arrand (10)
Crowle County Primary School, Nr Scunthorpe

THE GHOST OF THE HOUSE

'Mum, I've just seen the ghost.'
'What?'
'I've just seen the ghost. He's on the roof.'
'Oh darling, that's the repair man. He's mending our roof.'
'Oh good,' said Sarah.

This is a story about an eleven-year-old girl who rules the whole house. There is a ghost in this story who was killed three hundred years ago. At 12.00 midnight he comes out and rattles his chains.

'Sarah!' shouted her maid. Sarah is an eleven year old girl who rules the whole house.
'Yes,' said Sarah.
'The soldiers are here,' said the maid.
'Oh good, invite them in please,' said Sarah.

'Your ladyship,' said the boss of the soldiers.
'Follow me,' said Sarah, 'we'll go in the living room.'
'What's that big mark on the floor?' said one of the soldiers.
'That is blood,' said the maid very scared.
'Blood!' said Ben, who is one of the soldiers.
'A man got killed here three hundred years ago,' said the maid. 'He got bricked up behind that wall and died.'
'Well, I think I have just the thing that will get it off,' said another soldier.

He scrubbed it off . . . but the lights turned off and came back on; the blood stain started to come back. The maid fainted of shock.

At 12.00 midnight the ghost came out. He crept into Sarah's room and grabbed her, *aarrrr!*

Louise Ella (11)
Crowle County Primary School, Nr Scunthorpe

Menace Vs Menace

Early in the morning in the park there was a menace called Dennis. They were the worst of all menaces. No one could out menace them, but a boy and a dog came very close. I'll tell you the story.

One hot summer day in the park Dennis and Knasher were nowhere in sight. They weren't on the swings, they weren't playing rugby and everybody knew when they were not around. They were ready to strike then Dennis came through the gate with his hands behind his back. 'Hey, what's up?' he said.

Suddenly he swung his hands round with a two hundred hyper blaster in each hand and Knasher had a bag full of water bombs. 'Get 'em,' he shouted.

Splash, splosh. 'Leave 'em,' said a boy.
'Yeah! Who's gonna stop me?' Dennis said.
'I am,' said the boy.

Then he pulled out a three thousand hyper blaster and shot Dennis. Dennis laughed and shot him back. They both laughed. 'Hey, you're pretty good,' Dennis said.

After that they became best friends and menaced everybody in town. No one could stop them, and I mean no one. Well that's it, that's the story.

Karl Goulding (10)
Crowle County Primary School, Nr Scunthorpe

SPORTS

There was once a young boy called Tom and a young girl called Jessica.

'Oh hi Jessica,' said Tom.
'It's sports day in a week, do you want to practise with me?' said Jessica.
'Yeah, come on then we can start with jogging round Ealand,' said Tom.

It took them one hour to get round. They were exhausted after all that running but they didn't stop. They started jumping on trampolines. It started raining but that still didn't stop them either.

They went into the gym but after an hour they went out to go home. Then they went and had pizzas. A couple of days later it was sports day.

'Come on,' shouted Jessica. 'You've won.'
'It's your turn now,' said Tom. 'Go on, you can run.'

'Good on you Jessica, you got 3rd place,' said Tom.
'Come on, let's go and get an ice cream,' said Jessica.
'I'm getting a screwball. What are you getting?' said Tom.
'I will have a Fruit 5's,' said Jessica.
'Two then please,' said Tom to the ice cream man.
'£3 change,' said the ice cream man.

After they had their ice cream they went for the presentation.

Jessica got 3rd place and Tom got 1st place for the boys. They went up to collect their trophies. After they'd collected them they went home to have tea and then go to bed.

Sophie Grimbleby (10)
Crowle County Primary School, Nr Scunthorpe

Ghosts Vs Humans

'Welcome to the final between Ghosts and Humans. One team is full of ghosts!' shouted the commentator.

On the pitch the teams are doing their warm-ups. Now they get into their positions. The referee blows his whistle. You can't see the ghosts, only the football. They are invisible. The ball doesn't reach any human midfielder or striker, but the ghosts, who score.

Now the score is 1-0. The Humans just slide and hit the ball away and Seaman jumps and dives for the ball.

Now the second half begins. After one minute the ghosts start to become visible. The ball goes to Gerrard, Fowler and Beckham. They pass the ball to Owen and Heskey who have shots at the goal. Within twenty minutes they score two goals.

Just twenty-five minutes to be played. There, a ghost breaks through. Ferdinand stops him, passes the ball to Campbell, but a ghost intercepts the pass, takes a shot and scores an amazing goal. The score is 2-2.

One more minute to be played. Owen to Heskey, Heskey to Beckham, Beckham to Gerrard. *Goal!* Gerrard has just scored a last minute winner. Now they have the Cup!

Kieran Simpson (11)
Crowle County Primary School, Nr Scunthorpe

Football Mad

One day a ten-year-old boy was playing football in his garden. He was small, chubby and always in the fridge. His name's Paul. He played football for the school team.

Quick and fast he looked around the fence for his friends. Slim was as skinny as a stick, Speedy was fast and cool and Stinky always smelt awful.

Paul's mum and dad were always worried for some reason. Every time he went to the shop his parent worried after five seconds.

At school they had PE first period. The teacher went over to the four of them and said, 'We have a football match on Saturday this week and I would like you to play.'

Paul went home and told his parents who were nearly crying from being so worried; when he told them their faces went down even more. 'That is Grandma's birthday, you can't play,' they said.

At school the next day he told the teacher and the teacher said he understood. He would put Jack on instead. On Saturday the party poppers went off the same time as kick-off. Paul was crying and he was eating his food. As I said, he was always in the fridge.

Gareth Ambler (10)
Helpringham Primary School, Nr Sleaford

THE THREE-EYED FISH

One day I went fishing with my dad. My dad's a good fisher. When he was little he went fishing with his dad and his grandad. He caught a really big fish with a crabbing line and his dad and his grandad didn't catch anything, and they had proper fishing rods. Anyway, back to the real world. As I was saying, my dad's a good fisher.

I'm looking for some more worms; my dad is just putting a worm on my hook. I went back to my dad and started fishing; just then I saw something big move under the water, edging towards my float. When I saw my float go under I pulled and pulled. I quickly grabbed the net and pulled the thing out of the water.

Suddenly I realised that it was a three-eyed fish and this was not all, it was yelling at me. When it stopped it said, 'OK, OK, now listen up, I have to grant you three wishes, so get on with it.'

I wished for what anyone would wish for, to be rich and famous, my second wish was to end world hunger and I am saving the last wish for an emergency.

Oliver Jones (10)
Helpringham Primary School, Nr Sleaford

The Person Down The Stairs

Stuart woke with a start. He had had a nightmare. Someone had tried to kill him in it. He calmed down and lay there silently. He got up for the toilet and crossed the landing; something caught his eye moving at the bottom of the stairs. He ran to the light switch, turned it on, and then ran back to the stairs. There was a person; the person was not in his family.

Stuart called, 'Dad, come quickly.'

Dad instantly woke. The person ran into the nearest room from the stairs. Stuart ran downstairs, shutting the door into the room. He heard footsteps behind him. Stuart looked round, it was Dad. 'What's wrong?' wondered his dad.
'There's someone in this room,' whispered Stuart.

His dad got an umbrella from the hall stand, opened the door, turned the light on and the person had gone! However, the window was open. He walked across the room and closed it. 'Back to bed. I'll call the police,' said Stuart's dad.

Next morning Stuart's dad was reading the paper then he said, 'Yesterday a criminal escaped from Hanville.'
'That's probably the person who was here last night,' said Stuart.
'Probably,' said his dad.

Alec Vickerson (11)
Helpringham Primary School, Nr Sleaford

LEFT IN CHARGE

One day as the Queen was getting ready to go to Scotland, she found out she had not got a housekeeper, so she went to Mr Bean's house and said, 'Will you please be my housekeeper?'
'Yes,' said Mr Bean, 'I will.' And then Mr Bean said, 'When would you like me to start?'
The Queen replied, 'Today.'

Mr Bean was really excited and asked Her Majesty if she could take him in her limo because his car had broken down. The Queen agreed, so they got in the limo and went to Buckingham Palace.

When they arrived at the Palace they settled down and had a cup of tea. Mr Bean couldn't believe his luck, to think he was actually having tea with the Queen. Wow!

The Queen left for Scotland. Ten minutes later a robber stole a jewel. Mr Bean caught the robber by accident. He threw a banana skin at the robber's feet while he was trying to escape. The robber was sent to prison.

Mr Bean went to bed and the next day, at dinner time, the Queen came back. She said, 'How was the day?'

Mr Bean explained what happened and the Queen said he had to be called Sir Bean.

Jack Musson (11)
Helpringham Primary School, Nr Sleaford

THE TREASURE MAP

I studied the map again. It looked like a treasure map. I was sure I recognised parts of my town on it. Abi and Jo were close at hand and I'm sure Wayne (the geeky creep) was too.

'What is it?' they both shouted. Then we heard a loud clatter. 'Bet it's Wayne,' they panted, starting to move on.
'We need to head towards that old cave,' I muttered.
'Looking at my calculations, we should be there in exactly two hours,' Abi gabbled.
'Let's go to that waterfall and wash, we are outside the cave now,' Jo cheerfully said.

After a bit we were at the cave. 'Let's move while Wayne is not about,' I shouted.
Then Abi gave a loud scream and then came a voice, Wayne's voice. 'So this is where the treasure is,' he shouted raising a knife to Abi's neck. 'Give me the *map* or else!' he said even louder.
'Or else what?' Jo laughed.
'I'll kill her, that's what,' he said giving an awful cackle.
'How will you kill her if you are dead yourself?' I screeched.

Jo then whistled and Jasmine (my pet tiger) started to chase Wayne and we never heard or saw Wayne again.

Sophie Hurley (10)
Helpringham Primary School, Nr Sleaford

How The Cheetah Got His Spots

One sunny day a cheetah called Silma, a new cheetah in the jungle, asked his aunts and uncles how the Clueco bird got his colour.

'Uncle Monkey, how did the Clueco bird get his colour?' asked Silma, and Uncle Monkey smacked him on the head.
'Aunt Elephant, how did the Clueco bird get his colour?' and Aunt Elephant smacked him on the head.
'Uncle Hippo, how did the Clueco bird get his colour?' asked Silma, and Uncle Hippo smacked him on the head.

Silma was walking along a path in the jungle. He could hear the Clueco bird singing. He came to a tree. Silma looked up and saw the Clueco bird, 'Clueco bird,' Silma shouted. As Silma shouted the Clueco bird was painting a picture and all of the black paint spotted on the cheetah and that is how the cheetah got his spots.

So, we will never know how the Clueco bird got his colour, but we know how cheetah got his spots.

Joanna Fihelebon (11)
Helpringham Primary School, Nr Sleaford

The Two Wishes

'Zola scores again for Manchester United,' shouted Andy Gray.

Man United were into the Premiership final. After the match I went to Zola. 'I wish that I was the best footballers in the world,' I said excitedly.
'Do you know what?' Zola replied. 'I wish I am coaching you when you get into the Premiership final.'

11 years later . . .

'They've done it, they're into the 2061 Premiership final.'

'Try and score five goals in this match,' Zola said confidently.
'The only thing I need is to be the best footballer, because you are already my coach,' I replied.
'Just you do your best,' he said.

The match started. Liverpool in the first thirty minutes scored six goals, and looked the most likely for winning.

In the first minutes I scored and then in the 52nd and 56th, once more in the 66th, again in the 77th and the last in the 89th. The whistle went. What for? A handball, penalty to Man United.

Easily Van Nistelrooy placed it into the top right hand corner of the net. The whistle went, everybody cheered. We were the first team to win over thirteen Premiership finals.

'Well done!' Zola said.
'Now our wishes are true,' I said excitedly.

Jacob Wright (10)
Helpringham Primary School, Nr Sleaford

The Treasure Quest

Sarah was walking down the street when suddenly she tripped over a box. 'Mum, look! I've found a box on my way home.'
'Open it then,' said her mum.

As they opened it they saw a map that looked like their attic. They went upstairs to the attic to see if it matched the map. They started following the directions to see what they could find. As they were walking everything in the room moved. 'Mum, what's happening?'

Suddenly they turned around and saw a white figure in front of them. 'Leave my treasure or I will kill you!' it said.
By this time Sarah was crying. 'Mum, let's leave the treasure.'

Mum got some dust out of her pocket and the ghost disappeared.
'What's happened?'
'Ghosts are scared of dust. Keep looking.'

They had been looking for an hour. 'Mum, I'm tired. Can we stop now?'
'No, we've only got one more turn to do.'
They turned around and in front of them was a box that looked like a treasure chest. They opened it up and found millions of gold coins and started throwing them. 'We're rich!' Mum shouted.

From that day Sarah and her mum lived a wonderful life.

Abigail Jones (11)
Helpringham Primary School, Nr Sleaford

The Two Wishes

'Huh huh,' panted Joe and Max. 'We have been chased by overgrown lions, a killer frog and nearly killed by a quicksand monster, and we're still alive.'

But Max wasn't listening. He was too busy looking at the temple. 'Max, Max!' Joe shouted.

Joe looked up. Max couldn't get to sleep. He didn't know why. All of a sudden the door opened. Max woke Joe. They walked up to the door and went in.

There were bandages and bones everywhere. Then they saw it - the ball of osiers. Joe picked it up and the ball started talking, then it grew legs, arms and a head. Just then it said, 'I challenge you to a duel, If you win you get two wishes. If I win I get to suck out your soul. Here, I'll demonstrate on this person I kept as a slave. Now watch, and learn.'

'Ahh, help me!' screamed the old man.

Splat! His body was destroyed. Max wanted to back out but he stayed to fight. Joe said, 'We accept your challenge and with one strike of their sword the ball's head fell off but he grew another, but that fell off and he was defeated.

They each got their wishes. Joe wished for peace and Max wished that he could make the world a better place.

Joseph Spencer (9)
Helpringham Primary School, Nr Sleaford

My Gran And Me

We're on our way to the seaside in the car. When we get there we searched for a spot in the car park.

'Got one!'
'Moondust,' Gran said (that's Gran's favourite word for good.)

Gran is a short, plump woman with short bushy hair with lots and lots and lots of beads and bracelets.

'Come on Mia, let's go on the beach,' she said.

I am Mia. I am also short and thin with long hair and not many beads and bracelets.

Gran and I walked to the beach.

'Let's dig a hole as big as you Gran.' (As you can imagine that's very big!)
'Moondust!' said Gran happily.

Soon they began to dig and dig and dig and dig. They were very tired after that. 'Let's go for a paddle now Gran,' I shouted.
'Moondust!' Gran shouted back.

Gran and I got into our swimsuits. Splash, splash, splash!

'Gran, I would like an ice cream,' I said. So we got out of the water and went to have one.

'Bye sun. Bye sea. Bye sand,' I whispered when we left to go home.

Kathryn Herbert (10)
Helpringham Primary School, Nr Sleaford

Will They Take The Cup Home?

On the 31st it will start,
The World Cup is a kind of art,
With fantastic teams,
Everybody dreams,
That they will take the cup home.

With teams like France and Spain,
It will be a pain,
For the English team,
To reach their dream,
To take the cup home.

Who has the biggest ego?
Is it Beckham, Zidane or Figo?
I will bet that,
100s of shots will be in the back of the net,
Who will take the cup home?

Will England go the full mile
And win in style?
Will they win or will they lose,
It's up to them to choose,
If they take the cup home.

Will the fans have big parts
In the English teams hearts,
Are they bound?
To go to the second round,
And further to take the cup home.

Who will score?
To open the door,
So they go up,
Towards the cup,
Will they take the cup home?

In the final will they take the cup away
From the Frenchmen on the day?
They have made their way to glory,
And this is the end of the story,
They have, taken the cup home.

Robert Spencer (11)
Helpringham Primary School, Nr Sleaford

THE LIFE OF JOANNA

Joanna is my best friend. She is very funny. Joanna lives at 3 Barley Close, Heckington. I have known her for two years. She is a very nice friend.

Her mum and dad live in separate houses and most of the time I go to her dad's house. Joanna has four brothers. I've only met two though - they are very nice. Jo has a pet dog and a hamster. She loves to go shopping, especially when it's clothes shopping.

She has lots of jeans and tracksuit bottoms. Most of the time she wears trainers with those. New Look and Claire's Accessories are her favourite shops in Boston or Lincoln.

Joanna has brown hair with red streaks (only done on Wednesday 22nd May). Joanna has brown eyes. She loves to play netball, she plays goalkeeper. Sometimes she will come and play rounders, but her favourite all-time sport is netball.

Joanne is a very loyal friend. She is kind and will make you laugh if you're not feeling very well.

I am Joanna's best friend because she thinks that I am the same (loyal and kind.)

Sophie Floyd (10)
Helpringham Primary School, Nr Sleaford

The Life Of Bart Simpson

Hi, you may know me as Bart Simpson. I'm here to tell you about my life. Let me start with my family. I have two sisters called Maggie and Lisa, a crazy mum called Marge and a dad called Homer - he is addicted to *Duff Beer*.

Anyway, back to me. We have got a local shop. Homer has a local pub called Moe's Tavern and Marge has a job as a housewife. Lisa is a pupil at Springfield Elementary School.

I'm not a bad little boy but I get a bit naughty at times. My best object to play on is my skateboard. I go everywhere with it - it is my favourite!

Also, I have a dog called Santa's Little Helper. He used to be a racing dog but he's a house-dog now.

I live in America, in Springfield. I go to the same school as Lisa.

I have to go now, Dad is shouting my name.

Katie Prince (11)
Helpringham Primary School, Nr Sleaford

A Day In The Life Of A Rabbit

The name's Roger, Roger the rabbit. I've got two old owners, Margaret and Frank. I'm pretty sure they're over 80 (or even over 100!) Margaret is very nice, but she definitely doesn't look it. She looks as evil as me with those green eyes. Frank, on the other hand, looks really nice, but he isn't. He nearly killed me once. I had chewed his slippers (they were not very nice) and he was furious. He kicked me so hard I went flying and got stuck in the trees in our backyard. It took forever for him to get me down and I was getting mad. He finally grabbed me and we both fell with a big *thump!* I was not very happy.

I was out in Frank's vegetable patch and I was wondering if I would have a nibble of the carrots, when I heard something. I was not confident. I saw a long, fluffy brown tail. I went up to it. I couldn't believe my eyes. It was Will the weasel. He ran after me. I hid in the bushes. I saw him eat the vegetables. When he had finished eating, everything except the carrots, he was just about to go when I ran after him. He saw Margaret and Frank coming outside and ran off.

'Oh Roger! How could you?' snapped Margaret. 'You naughty rabbit.'

Liam Summers (10)
Lord Deramore's Primary School, York

A Day In The Life Of Chandler The Hamster

It was Monday morning and I was going to school in my ball with Stuart. I didn't know what school was but it sounded fun. I got my breakfast, I cleaned myself and ran around in my wheel for a bit.

'I'm going,' Stuart shouted and he picked me up in my ball.

It was a bumpy ride going to school because he took his bike. It was very big, it had a chain and some pedals and some big wheels.

When we got to school we had a wait in this big place, so he let me run about for a bit until it got crowded.

When we got in the building this teacher kept saying people's names. The teacher let me run about on the table in my ball. I almost fell off. I was running about happily until I needed a wee-wee. I couldn't hold it. Then, oh dear! Wee squirted out of the air holes and all over Stuart. He didn't look very happy, neither did the teacher. Then suddenly, *'Rar rar rar!'* went the teacher. I shrivelled into the back of my ball and closed my ears so I couldn't hear.

At lunch I had go to home because the teacher said I caused too much mayhem, so Stuart had to take me home and put me in my cage.

Angus Vasili (10)
Lord Deramore's Primary School, York

A Day In The Life Of A Wasp

Why can't people understand? I'm a wasp. I'd better start from the beginning.

One day I was getting pollen from flowers, just like any other normal wasp would do, right? Then I flew through an open window into a house, just like any other wasp would do. All right, maybe not. But I thought it was an extra big beehive or something.

Anyway, as soon as I flew in, I looked around and immediately tried to fly out again, but I couldn't. Why? Because one of the big humans had shut the window. If they didn't want me here they should let me out. I went head first into the glass - double-glazed too! That made me really angry. I started flying about looking for an exit. Not only wasn't there one, but one of the humans almost sat on me, that made me even more angry.

Then one of them noticed me and they all started swatting at me with a rolled up newspaper while clapping. One of them almost got me. That made me the angriest wasp around. I stung the biggest one on the cheek. He screamed. Well, it's his own fault.

A woman opened the door and I flew through her legs and out. I narrowly escaped with my life.

Itamar Lavidor (10)
Lord Deramore's Primary School, York

A Day In The Life Of A Parrot

'Food!' I told Billy. Billy gave me a big slice of fruit. I ate my fruit.
Then Billy started telling me, 'Shut up, shut up, shut up!'
I answered him, 'Shut up, water.' Billy gave me some water. 'Shut up,' I told him.

I started thinking how to escape. I got my beak through the metal bars and saw something sparkling. I pushed it. The door opened so I flew out. It was wonderful, although at first I forgot how to fly and dropped onto the floor. But soon I remembered and was flying across the room. I flew into the kitchen and saw some brown stuff, so I nibbled it. It was the best stuff I had ever tasted. I dragged it in the cage.

Billy saw me. 'Shut up!' I told him and flew on. Then I went into a room I'd never seen before. There was a tap and a strange thing with a handle. I sat on the handle - *vroom!* it went. I flew out and went into the kitchen and got some of the brown stuff and pulled the sparkling thing. There was a big fuss. I didn't understand anything but when Billy wanted the brown stuff I said, 'Shut up!' and started nibbling.

Yasha Tchetchik (9)
Lord Deramore's Primary School, York

A Day In The Life Of A Puppy

Why, why, why do they have to smack me? Anyway, it was only a trickle. If they had taken me for a walk then it would not have happened.

'You bad, bad, bad dog,' he shouted at me. They still have not thought of a name for me, but I think it must be Bad Dog. The best thing though, was that they tied me outside. It was wonderful. I made a new friend as well. I thought to myself, if I could get away from those awful owners of mine . . . but then they took me inside and they got me a nice warm blanket. When the big boy had gone I went for a wander around the room I was in.

There was a big, round circular thing which spun around (washing machine) and there was a big, tall, white thing (fridge-freezer) which was warm at the bottom, so I moved my blanket under it and just laid next to it.

When the big circular thing (washing machine) stopped turning, the lady, who the boy calls Mum, came in and said, 'How are you doing Milo?' Then I thought maybe Milo was my name.

She walked up to the washing machine and took out some more blankets and walked back out of the room. I went and put my blanket in and let it spin around and around. I don't know why, but then Mum came in and said to me, 'Oh, how clever you are!' Then she took out my blanket and said goodnight.

I put my blanket under the warm thing and went to sleep thinking about what I would do next morning.

Sophie Wright (10)
Lord Deramore's Primary School, York

A Day In The Life Of Bob The Mouse

Hi, I'm Bob. Incase you hadn't noticed I'm a mouse. Anyway, I got into a fight with a cat. I gave him a good bit of rough and tumble. After some time I beat seven shades of brain out of him.

Getting back to present day, the old hag from number forty-two is moping about. I roughed up her cat, Whiskers. Come on, doesn't anyone watch Tom and Jerry around here? Jerry beats Tom every day. Now if I go anywhere near the house, I find lots of broomsticks flying down at me.

I decided I would go for some cheese so I ran off to the house. I spotted a cardboard box and decided I would treat myself to a nibble. I ran off when I heard a purr from a cat inside, before it got me. Although it took me a long time, it was worth it, or I thought it was.

When I got in the house there was a mousetrap. I was an expert at dodging them so I grabbed the cheese and ran - *snap!* The trap shut and got my tail. Then Whiskers approached me. There was nothing I could do. He opened his jaws, saliva dripping from his teeth, I held my breath - *snap!*

Christopher Whiting (10)
Lord Deramore's Primary School, York

A Day In The Life Of A Tiger

Hate it, hate it, hate it - children pressing their ugly faces on the window. Honestly, they make such a fuss and make such a loud noise that I can never sleep at night and day, Oh and the food, it's so bad, I would rather have no food at all. It's the same every day, meat chunks.

Anyway, what an exciting day I've had. It was this morning when the zoo keeper, Ben, got me out of my cage and took me for a walk. Suddenly the clip snapped and that was where the excitement started.

I was free, I really was! It was amazing, but the people who were visiting didn't find it the slightest bit amazing. They were all screaming, even a little girl tried to climb a lamp post but failed. Luckily she had an ice cream - chocolate, vanilla, strawberry, fudge and jam, yummy. I scared her away and she dropped her ice cream, so I just grabbed it.

Now I was the boss, not some dopey old child. I let the monkeys, hyenas, rhinos, giraffes, zebras and birds out of their cages. I felt really good, but Ben did not seem very impressed at all. He was bright red in the face. All the guests were leaving, so I decided to make a run for it. I ran through the barn and park towards the gate, but the gate was closed. Ben caught me by the ear and dragged me to my cage.

After all the commotion, I felt tired so I went to sleep.

Lucie Berry (10)
Lord Deramore's Primary School, York

A Day In The Life Of A Killer Cat

All right, all right I admit it, I killed a bird but what do you expect from me? I'm a cat. You don't expect me just to leave it and go away. It just came down and flew in my mouth. Well, I'm a cat and I ate it, so what? I spat it back out again after I'd eaten all of the feathers. I spat out the bones too. I brought the bones into the house and left them on the carpet. There were bloodstains everywhere. I got shouted at. Polly just got all soppy. 'Oh Sasha, how could you?'

Yeah, yeah, I just thought. How could I? Whatever!

Eventually the fuss was over and we had a funeral for the poor, old, sad bird. Polly got a box and put all of the bones inside. You could hear them go crunch! Polly said a silly old prayer and how sorry she was that I'd killed it. Whatever, I just thought, yeah, yeah. Can we just finish this silly old funeral? Polly put the box in the mud and got out the shovel and buried him. After it was all finished they went back inside. I wasn't allowed in though.

When it was bedtime I still wasn't allowed back in and had to sleep in the cold breeze in a cage.

Adam McMahon (10)
Lord Deramore's Primary School, York

A Day In The Life Of Sandy the Dog

Today started with me waking up and yawning. I stretched and jumped onto the bed lying next to Mum and Dad - well, Charlotte's mum and dad. I started to lick Mum's face then Dad's. Dad shouted at me to get off the bed so I jumped down and started to pee. I always pee because Charlotte comes and feels sorry for me. She didn't this time. I just got shouted at.

I ran downstairs and looked in my dish, nothing there! So I yowled and yowled until Charlotte came down. I stared up at her and then into my bowl and waited. Charlotte put some biscuits in it. I stared up at her as if to say, you don't actually expect me to eat that? She went to play on the computer so I went into the living room to chew my chew. Dad took me out for a walk in the fields. *It was really cool!*

When I got back I found a *rat in the garden.* I could not believe it. I chased it around the garden and finally caught it. Then I ran around with my trophy until Dad saw the rat and shouted. I quickly ran upstairs and buried it in Mum and Dad's bed.

I played with Nel all afternoon - well, that is until Dad went to bed. I had forgotten about the rat, so I ran upstairs but it was too late. I heard the scream when I was on the top step. I decided to go downstairs and look all cute and innocent in my basket. But it didn't work. I had to sleep outside for the night.

Charlotte Cooper (9)
Lord Deramore's Primary School, York

SQUEAKY'S GREAT ESCAPE

My name is Squeaky and I wish I wasn't trapped in this cage all the time. 'Yeah! It's ball time,' I squeaked in my tiny voice as my master came with the ball.

'In you go!' His big booming voice went as I slipped into the ball . . . *Ding dong,* rang the doorbell, and I quickly ran in my ball to the door. The door opened, I took my chance and jumped out. Oh no! I was caught by none other than my master.

'Please, no, let me go now!' I squeaked as loudly as I could. Huh! The door to my ball had opened and I jumped out to freedom. Boom, boom, boom - my master was running after me.

'Waaahh!' I squeaked as I fell through a drain into the sewers. Down and down I fell until . . *thud!* I fell onto a concrete floor.
'Ow, that was hard wasn't it?' Came another squeak and a big black rat appeared from the shadows.
'Yeah!' I replied quite weakly. I was hurt, badly. 'Have you got any shelter I can rest in?' I asked.
'Of course I have,' he replied in a jolly voice and I followed him - limping. 'Have you got a name? I'm Ratty.'
'Yeah, I'm Squeaky,' I replied as I began my new life.

Dean Dunn (10)
Lord Deramore's Primary School, York

A Day In The Life Of Milo The Puppy

'Milo, get in your bed while we have breakfast,' Mum shouted.

I'm Milo, as you might know already. That was my mum telling me off. I don't know why? Just because I'm wandering about while they're eating I suppose.

I'm waiting for my walk. The little one is jumping around shouting, 'Can we take Milo for a walk? Can we please?' And I'm nearly making myself desperate for the toilet, I'm so excited. My walk is waiting for me. We're going to walk near the river. I love it down there. My lead is off now. They throw my ball. But what's that in the river? A duck!

Splash! I was in after, I think you can guess, the duck. After a few minutes I brought the duck out, but dead. Okay, okay, spank me, do whatever now. I was all muddy and wet with a dead duck at my feet.

They took the duck home, I got told off for killing the bird, plus jumping on their cream sofa, or now cream and brown. I got shut outside in the cold. But then they came out with a box and spade. In the box was the duck. Dad dug a hole and put the box in it. We had to have a funeral for the duck, and I had to sit and watch.

Jodie Ridsdale (10)
Lord Deramore's Primary School, York

A Day In The Life Of Twinkle The Dog

Oh shoot me! I just sent a human into hospital with bad cuts and bruises. I do it nearly every day. They know I'm coming because I stalk them before I do it. There's one person who has never gone into hospital. His name is Tom. I've jumped on him, I've bitten him but he never goes into hospital.

I live with Tom and I sleep in his room sometimes. I really cheese him off by weeing on his carpet as it stinks, but if I do it I get chucked outside. I do it for fun because I just sleep in the shed.

I really cheesed Tom off once when I ripped his teddy limb from limb. Then I got a really big smack which hurt quite a lot and my bum went bright pink. Then I got my own back. I went downstairs and I waited till Tom came down. Suddenly I pounced on him, then it happened, Tom had to go in hospital with a claw in his stomach.

Thomas Johnson (10)
Lord Deramore's Primary School, York

A Day In The Life Of A Rat

Who cares? For heaven's sake, all I did was bite a tiny little hole in Dad's new shirt which he got for a Christmas present. He was lucky enough to get presents, I didn't get anything. I got yelled at and was practically thrown into my cage. It wasn't my fault, Laura left my cage open when she was feeding me. They should try being locked in a small cage all day. He can buy a new shirt anyway.

Okay, I admit it, it was me who bit the hole in the carpet and it was me who bit a hole in Mum and Dad's mattress. There's no need to pick me up and then squeeze me so tight, I almost died, and then there's not feeding me for ages.

It's not fair! I don't see anybody else in this house getting punished for a crime they didn't commit, not even the pet cat, he does more bad stuff than me.

He was the one who flattened all the flower beds and it was him who threw up on the living room carpet. He didn't even get told off. I don't know why they even keep a rat. They don't know how to look after one properly. It seems like they want to sell me and buy a different pet. Anyway, Dad's walking over and it looks like I'm in trouble, so bye.

Lauren Beadnell (10)
Lord Deramore's Primary School, York

A Day In The Life Of Tweet The Parrot

All right, all right, I'm stupid. But they were making such a fuss about the vicar coming.

'Polly, Polly have you brushed your hair properly?' or 'Polly, get that lovely pink dress of yours and wear that.' But Polly didn't have the worst of it.

First Mrs Neat woke me, at 6am! She washed me twice, rubbed rose smelling soap down my feathers and combed my feathers again and again. And then it got worse. She tied a tiny pink pinny round my waist and attached a small bonnet on my head.

Mr Neat had his best clothes on because Mrs Neat had forced him to. I heard her screaming, 'Neil, they're horrid those jeans! Scruffy they are, what's the vicar going to think?'
She'll think what a family! I would. A parrot in a pinny, it's sickening.

The vicar arrived in a tiny black skirt and a huge black woolly jumper. I, acting all good at the moment, swept down to her and pecked her ear. She giggled at this, yuck!

They all sat down to chicken casserole, roast potatoes and Yorkshire puddings - lucky people. I had to have fruit and nuts.

They had all just finished when I decided it was time. I shouted (or rather squawked) at the top of my voice, 'Mrs Neat has a huge wart on her bottom.' It's true though, hang me. The vicar fainted. It was not that terrible, but it was true, true! Polly and Mr Neat couldn't help chuckling.

Now I'm out in the garden. Chucked out for awhile. Although Polly threw out some lovely chicken and a bit of Yorkshire pudding - better than fruit and nuts.

Rachel Lovelady (10)
Lord Deramore's Primary School, York

A Day In The Life Of A Cat

Okay, okay, I may have killed a rat and I did bring it into the house, but what do you expect? I'm a cat and I saved the house. It was trying to get in, it could have hurt me, let alone wrecked the house. Luckily I was there.

I thought I would get a reward for it but all I got was a hit over the head, it hurt too. They were so upset, they had a gravestone and buried it in the garden. I was not allowed to go and I knew the rat when he was alive.

Okay, okay, I may have killed a bird but I was hungry and it was just a little one. Guess what, I got another hit over the head and the bird had a gravestone too. Now I am not allowed out of the house and the other cats laugh at me, but I guess I will have to put up with it.

Jordan Coulson (10)
Lord Deramore's Primary School, York

A Day In The Life Of A Parrot

Hi, I'm Polly. I'm no ordinary parrot who asks for crackers. No! I'm a naughty parrot who cheeks people back and calls them names. I'm multicoloured and I think I'm beautiful.

'Polly come and get your bird seed,' said Kim.
'Orrr ,orrr, I'm coming, I'm coming,' I said.
'Come on Kim, bedtime,' said Kim's mum.

It was eleven o'clock by now and everyone was fast asleep. Now was my chance to escape. My cage door was open so I flew out quickly. I was sneaking around looking for something to eat when the doorbell went. It was Gran and Grandad. Dad opened the door and he was rubbing his eyes to see who it was.

'Good morning son. How are you? See, we need somewhere to stay because we've got a big hole in our roof so could we stay the night please?' said Grandad kneeling on his knees.
'Of course you can,' said Dad in a sleepy way.

Dad switched on the night light.

'Oh no!' I said. I dashed to the cupboard, but it was shut. Luckily the window was open so I flew out. There was a storm and by now it was one in the morning. I was tapping on the window, 'Let me in.'

Everyone woke up. They all came downstairs. 'What is it? Oh, it's only Polly. How did you get out there?' Dad said.

Kimberley Bostock (9)
Lord Deramore's Primary School, York

A DAY IN THE LIFE OF PATCH THE HAMSTER

Look at them, staring at me going, 'He's so cute!' Yuck. I'm going to throw up. It's so boring too. Uh oh, Emily's going to lift me out of the cage. I'm trying to run away but I can't. *I'm caught!*

I've been put in one of those stupid plastic balls. They want me to crawl around, but I'm not going to satisfy them.

Ding dong. 'I'll get it!' Emily's rushing to the door. This is my chance. Freedom calls me! I'm pushing the front of the ball with great effort. Yes, I've made it, I'm out.

Now, what chaos can I cause? Aha, the kitchen. Emily's family is one that has everything in order, especially the food.

I'm scampering around as quietly as I can, being careful. I'm in. I'm trotting along until - ow! I've banged into the bin. Okay, okay, and I've knocked it over and spilt all the rubbish - Oops! Great my ball's open!

I've jumped up onto a chair, then onto the kitchen counter. A cupboard is slightly open . . . packets ripped open, knocked over, spilling onto the floor, glass jars tipped and smashed, shards of glass everywhere!

A hamster's on the rampage! Emily's mum has walked in and screamed her head off. I'm put straight back into my cage, leaning back against the bedding.

This is the life, I'm thinking, yeah!

Amy Muckersie (10)
Lord Deramore's Primary School, York

A Day In The Life Of George The Mouse

Another day stuck in this old cage, eating the same food and going round in the same wheel. Boring! I've always dreamed of getting out of this stuffy cage. My owner, Andrew, never takes me out to play, he's too caught up being cool. I wish I could stay in the kitchen all day and fill my face with food, but that never happens.

He's coming over, he's opened my cage. Whoopie! Andrew's taking me out. I'm free. I quickly run off to the kitchen so he couldn't catch me again.

First I nibbled at the wood, then I headed straight for the cupboards. I saw food, lots of food. I went for the rice, it was delicious. Then I pulled at the cloth hanging from the ceiling. Suddenly the cloth fell down and I scampered out. I tried some wood, it was lovely. I ate lots of it. Then the chair leg fell off. Then I ripped up the carpet. This was such fun. I dragged off the wallpaper. Then Andrew's mum came in.

'What have you done? That mouse is going!'

Faye Garland (9)
Lord Deramore's Primary School, York

A SHADOW IN THE FOREST

'Come on everybody,' urged Jade. 'It's really going to be fun.'
'Oh yeah, it's heaven isn't it? Just what I need. Bogs, marshes - the list of wonders is endless!' remarked Jessica.
Her twin sister, Jasmine, agreed. 'Yeah, better than a bloomin' holiday in the Caribbean.'
Jo looked at them with a murderous glint in her eye. 'I'm warnin' you two,' she snarled, 'one more word . . .'

They took the hint and fell silent, but not for long.

'Look!' they squeaked simultaneously. Then everybody saw: a black shadow was circling the tent very, very slowly.

'Right, when it's round the other side we unzip the tent and run for our lives,' commanded Jo. '1, 2, 3, now!'

I ran - we all ran, over rocks and under branches. I landed on a patch of mud and started sliding down a hill. I couldn't see the others, but that didn't matter. All that mattered was getting away from that . . . that thing! I skidded to a halt at the bottom of the hill, breathless. I heard the sound of silence, the sound of peace but then the silence was broken.

Natalie Clarke (10)
Lord Deramore's Primary School, York

ORIENTEERING

'What should we do now then?' I asked.
'Oh stop moaning, I know which way it is,' Elizabeth replied.
I knew she was kidding. 'Which way then? There's just sheep, sheep and sheep to the west, a never ending road to the south and some more sheep to the east and . . .'
Elizabeth interrupted, 'I think we should go north into the forest.'

We were already halfway through and hadn't found anything.

'Look, look that owl again. I think its following us,' Elizabeth excitedly said. 'I think it's following us.'
'We've seen that owl a thousand times,' I informed her. 'That's because we're going round in circles.'
'No, not the owl. Look, look!' she shouted.

We both turned around carefully and nervously. 'Ahh!' we both screamed.

Rebekah Hattee (10)
Lord Deramore's Primary School, York

Shelter In The Dark

'Oi, Barbie doll,' shouted Kelly. 'Hurry up with those twigs.'
'Don't call me Barbie doll, I like Sindy!' said Emma, struggling with a bundle of twigs.
'And you, Racoon Face! I want those logs pronto!' commanded Kelly.

Kelly bound twigs together with a bit of rope she found. Declan brought the logs and Kelly tied the twigs to them. It was a bit cramped but at least it was shelter from the fierce weather outside.

Finally night came and it was time to sleep. Kelly stayed up and watched for unexpected appearances, but after two hours she fell asleep.

'Arrooww!'
'What was that?' screamed Emma.
Declan hushed her and all three sat stiff and listened. They had all woken with a start.

'I'll go out,' Kelly offered. Nobody stopped her. She crept out and looked around. Six black, big, wild dogs stared at her. She screamed. Declan and Emma came rushing out and stood, staring at the beasts. The dogs' bright yellow eyes glowed in the dark night.

'After three we run in the opposition direction - one, two, three!' They ran. Branches whipped their faces, blood trickled, feet ached and clothes ripped. They ran and ran for their lives. The dogs chased after them. They could hear their legs pounding on the dead leaves. Finally they came to a clearing. They stopped and turned - no dogs.

'Thank God that's over!' choked Declan.
Kelly looked around. 'Look, look! I can see a village,' she said excitedly.
'It's like ours!' Emma exclaimed.
'That's because it is ours!' shouted Declan.

Once again they ran, but it all stopped when they heard a voice. *'What are you doing on my property, you little brats!'*

They turned, behind them stood a grumpy looking man. His feet crunched through the leaves. He certainly wasn't going to let them go in a hurry.

Lorna Stillie (11)
Lord Deramore's Primary School, York

Fear

Danielle stared at the TV programme in a small bedroom. Teddy bears glanced all around the room watching every small movement. The shelves were rotten and damp because of a crack hiding behind an old, dusty ship. A lamp in the corner glimmered and faded away every passing second. The small TV that she stared at sat on an old stool which had a leg removed. The only seat was a weak, cold bed that dug into the fiery red coloured carpet.

It was an old house which was owned by two strange men. Danielle had been phoned by one of the men to babysit for a while.

The baby was fast asleep in a big bare room which had an ear-piercing squeak coming from the door. A loud voice came from the TV, but it was overcome from a loud noise from downstairs.

Her blood pumped around her body to fast and made her choke. Her head froze and then started to burn like an inferno. She went to the stairs. An old door was abandoned behind a big cloak hanger where lots of cloaks hung on. Danielle ran down the stairs.

She suddenly heard the baby cry but she dare not go back. She ran into the kitchen, knives were all glimmering. She ran out of the back door and tripped over the step. She looked up and with the glint of what she saw, she screamed.

Scott Sellars (11)
Lord Deramore's Primary School, York

STRANDED

'Help!' I screamed. It was quiet, no one answered. I was alone. The rocks were slowly crumbling. The rope was out of reach. I was swaying along, only one hand to hold me up - one hand to save my life. Suddenly I heard an unfamiliar voice - I had no idea who it was but I really didn't care.

'Help!' I shouted. It was silent. Maybe it was just my imagination running wild. My head was spinning around like a merry-go-round. My heart was beating so loud that I could hear it through my head. I felt abandoned, rejected, alone. The heat was draining out of my body - the only heat I had left in me. The rocks dug into my hands, blood trickled down my arm.

I felt like a rejected ship, slowly sinking into the depths of the ocean. No one nor nothing could help me. I tried to work my way up, but it was no use. I wished that Nadia and Jessica were here. Maybe they were - I tried to look up, but I couldn't see anything, all I could hear was the lashing of waves. I imagined myself falling, falling amongst the waves With rocks below me. I imagined sea creatures surrounding me, me drifting. I wished wishes could come true . . .wished . . . wishes . . .

My arms ached with exhaustion. I wanted to let go. I wanted to be someone else. My hand started sweating. I slowly lifted my fingers. I let go . . .

Busi Moon (11)
Lord Deramore's Primary School, York

WHAT IS IT?

I stared at the top of the tent. A funny smell attracted my nose. A howling and screeching noise from outside made my heart skip a beat.

I turned on the torch beside my sleeping bags. Howling and screeching still echoed on the tent and a shadowy figure appeared as I shone the light against the tent side.

I stepped out, it was pitch-black, but with the help of my torch I got a bit of light. I went further out, my tent slowly disappearing as I went away.

Smells and noises suddenly came from the tent. I ran back, my heart pumping as fast as light. I opened the tent zip. Nothing there, just my bag. I tried getting back to sleep but couldn't. The smell got worse and worse. Again another noise caught my ear. The figure came closer and closer to the tent. It was right near now. A claw appeared scrolling down into my tent. My face turned white. The claw got deeper and deeper into the tent side.

I jumped out of the tent like a kangaroo. My dad was there playing a trick on me, with a fake wolf mask on and fake claws. Typical!

Greg Lawn (11)
Lord Deramore's Primary School, York

Spooky Camp

The car was revving, ready to jerk forward. Mum stood at the door waving goodbye. My teeth were chattering against the window. Dad's blue eyes stared at me through the car mirror. A rumble came from a lorry passing by. I began to catch a view of the camp sign. *'Welcome to Brimpsten Activity Camp'* I read as we passed it. 'See you on Thursday kids,' Dad said grumpily.

Soon a woman with a short gold skirt on came and linked hands with me and Reece. She led us to our dormitory. It was a small but cosy room, I was feeling homesick and wanted to be at home so badly. That night I tossed and turned, drops of tears streamed down my face like a waterfall.

The next day we went into the hall. Kev and Lisa were there smiling at Reece. 'Someone's got an admirer,' I said to Reece.
'We are now going to go into the wood to find the Easter eggs,' said Miss Riggs.

The wood was darker than at the camp. All we had was torches. I was chatting to Kev about hating it at the camp when there as a blood-curdling scream coming from the river nearby. We ran over to it. There was no one there. Then someone pushed me in. I hit the water. I couldn't breath . . .

Jasmine Tubridy (10)
Lord Deramore's Primary School, York

Adventure Camp

Bump! We landed on a big hill. Our mission to find our president.

'Ah, help!'
'That must be the president!' Hugo exclaimed.
'Who?' replied Chiz looking confused.
'The president, come on!' Hugo exclaimed (who was already halfway down the hill.)

They lost track completely, they were about ten miles off track.

'What's that?' Chiz asked.
'That's the house we're looking for . . . yippee!' Hugo exclaimed.
'There's the door,' Chiz said.

Hugo reached for the door. He touched the handle . . . *slam!* Hugo had a quiver of shock. He stepped towards the sound with his torch. Then he tripped and lost the torch. He got on his hands and knees. He groped around on the floor, he could feel the paving slabs as he was scraping and groping around.

After five minutes of scrambling and groping around, finally he touched the metal of the torch, but it was a pole. Next to it was the torch. The batteries were flat. He could just work out the outlines of a few objects and a switch. He flicked it on. He froze and saw a big black shadow slip through the crack of the door.

Gavin Himsworth (11)
Lord Deramore's Primary School, York

CURSED CAMP

'Lynne, Lynne, what's that?' I trembled. I turned around, she wasn't there.

Crunch! Something or someone was out there. Should I go out? A howling noise echoed through the wood. Where was Lynne? Should I go out? What was it? I shone my torch outside. Blood was on the ground - tiny red droplets. Where was Lynne?

My heart skipped a beat. The wind whistled through the trees. Butterflies in my stomach, I jerked, knowing something was going to happen. My knees trembled. My knuckles were white. I started to sweat. My head was whizzing around like a whirlwind. All the questions I had to answer.

I heard the howling noise once again. I darted inside my tent and zipped up the tent door, crawled inside my sleeping bag and I curled up with my teddy bear. I tried to forget it and hoped it was a dream.

Gradually I peeled off my sleeping bag, still clutching my teddy bear. I had to be brave and go outside. Lynne was still not back. I picked up my torch, unzipped the tent and crawled outside, testing my wit. Who or what was out there?

I shone my torch outside. I slowly drew back the door. I shone the torch round again to see . . . Lynne clutching a wolf's mask and ketchup. It was her all along.

Lucy Thompson (11)
Lord Deramore's Primary School, York

My Adventure

'This is just great!' moaned Clare. 'Here we are stuck in the middle of nowhere with dumbo here.'
'Come on, help me set up the camp,' Emma said persuasively.
'Why should I help you set up your camp? I'm going to make mine,' said Clare with an evil look on her face. Clare pulled a face at her behind her back.

What was that? It was very late and Clare was woken up by a noise - a thumping noise next to her tent. She grabbed a torch and put on her shoes. She went out to look to see if dumbo or Emma were awake but they were fast asleep.

Clare shone the torch around to see what was there. She heard a snap of a crack twig behind her. Her heart missed a beat. Her blood froze. She counted to three in her head, 1, 2, 3. She quickly turned around. Nothing was there. Her head was spinning around like a washing machine.

Clare ran and climbed up a tree. She felt safe there. She tried to turn around on the tree but slipped. Her hands were holding onto the tree trunk and her wrists were twisted. She turned them around. Her hand slipped and her knuckles were white from holding on. Her arm was bleeding and her whole body was sweating. With only one arm to hold on with, her hand slipped and she fell into the darkness.

Hannah Dolling (11)
Lord Deramore's Primary School, York

A Day In The Life Of A Naughty Dog

Go! I just don't know why they found me and took me to their house if they don't like me. I'll tell you my fake owner's name. It is Laura and her angry dad Nick. He slaps me, he does everything just because I go out to play and come home to jump on the bed. If adults are allowed to do trampolining, why aren't I allowed to jump on the bed? I'm the one who's saving their time, not going out.

'Gary darling, I'm home.' That's Laura's mum. 'What have you done?' I tried to be nice but she said, 'It doesn't matter cutie pie.'
Nick came upstairs and shouted, 'You are going to be locked up for your whole life!'

The next morning he locked me up and went to work. I'll find a way out, I thought. When Lucy heard him say about locking me up she quickly got some pillows and play equipment, so I could have fun. I kept looking to see if there was a way out then suddenly there was a big hole that I could go through.

The next morning I had a brilliant plan. At night I pooed all over, by accident, the toilet and that wasn't my plan. It was for me to bite Nick, but who cares? Later, when he got home from work, he went to the toilet and all his glasses broke into pieces.

That's what I wanted to do!

Maahvash Hassib (10)
Lord Deramore's Primary School, York

A Day In The Life Of A Hamster

Hi, my name is Hammy and I am a hamster. I live in a cage with a wheel and tunnels, and a maze at the bottom. The bad things about living in a cage are I have the same food every day and I don't have a chance to run about.

I had a great idea of how to escape. As soon as they picked me up I ran and ran as fast as I could. I ran through the cat flap into the world (well actually the garden.) The cat was in the garden. I ran past the cat to this picnic mat. It had human food on so I went up to it and I nibbled at it - it was good. I nibbled and nibbled and nibbled. When I had finished I couldn't run.

I saw the door open and then I heard, 'Oh Hammy, that was our picnic. Where is the chocolate cake?' I was picked up. I couldn't run. They took me inside and I was locked up in my cage again.

David Crawshaw (10)
Lord Deramore's Primary School, York

George And The Cheese

'Bad boy,' Charlie yelled, 'stop it.'

Charlie was eleven years old and had a pet mouse called George. George was like one million little boys waiting to be fed - he was always so hungry. He was extremely fat and stank of garlic, although he never ate any! 'I said stop it,' screamed Charlie, 'get away from the cheese!' But, George did not do as he was told and kept nibbling away at the cheese.

Unexpectedly, he fell through the hole in the cheese that he had just eaten and disappeared. Charlie ran over to the cheese and tried to pull George out . . . but he was stuck. Suddenly, Charlie had an idea, he called, 'You're going to have to eat your way out!'

So, as if George understood Charlie, he started munching away again. A couple of hours later George was free, but he was even fatter now and had to go on a diet, which he was not very pleased about. But he learned his lesson - to do as he was told.

Ian Dawson (11)
Nafferton Primary School, Driffield

No Way Out

'I've got a bad feeling about this, mumbled Joanne. As they opened the mouldy door they heard laughter coming from upstairs.
'Who's that?' demanded Jamie.
Ha, ha, ha - Chloe ran quickly and squeezed Jamie.
'I'm scared,' shivered Chloe.
'You'll be fine,' muttered Joanne.
'We won't be fine! What if we get stuck inside this house?' yelled Jamie.
'We won't, we'll get out the way we came in,' screeched Joanne.

So they went to see if they could get out (the way they came in) which was through the front door. It didn't work. They tried smashing the window and leaping through it, but that wasn't successful either. They tried everything, but nothing worked.

'We're going to die of starvation,' sobbed Chloe pathetically.
Joanne quickly interrupted, 'We're not! I know we'll find something like a secret passage . . .'
Jamie started crying, 'We are going to *die* and it's all mine and Chloe's fault, regardless of the fact that you should have stopped us but . . . I'm sorry Joanne.'
Joanne whispered, 'It's OK.'
They all gave each other a hug and hoped someone would find them.

Terri Gascoigne (11)
Nafferton Primary School, Driffield

The Stolen Plate

'What is it?' asked David.
'It's some sort of gold plate, I wonder what it's doing here?' said Jack.
They picked it up and examined it.
'It could be a piece of treasure from hundreds of years ago,' suggested David.

The plate shone like the sun and had a picture of a dragon on it.
The dragon's face was an evil monster with scales all over. It was beautifully carved into the plate. It had been hidden in a pile of dirt, just outside the new building site!

David asked what he should do with it. Jack said, 'Let's ask someone else and see if they know whose it is.'
So with the plate under one arm they set off. They asked at the post office, but they could not help.

'What now?' whispered David.
'Let's go and play football on the school pitch,' supplied Jack quickly.
'OK,' said David.

On the way to the football pitch they passed the newsagent and they stood still, staring at the board, for on it was a notice saying:

Stolen Plate
Worth £20,000
£200 reward to finder.

David Lund (10)
Nafferton Primary School, Driffield

LOUISA'S LESSON

'Why do I have to?' cried Louisa, blood driving round her body like a racing car at the Grand Prix.
'Because if you expect to have your favourite strawberry pie you need to pick strawberries from the garden,' Louisa's mother cried, astonished at her daughter's behaviour.

Louisa's mother was a reasonable lady. In Louisa's opinion, picking strawberries was a pointless act and she preferred playing with friends. Slowly she went to the garden and was just about to pick a strawberry when a smartly dressed girl swung open the garden gate. 'Hi,' Louisa mumbled. It was Mary, her friend. Louisa muttered, 'Let's go . . .'
'What about the strawberries?' Mary proclaimed.
'Forget the strawberries,' Louisa whispered, for fear of her mother overhearing. Louisa went to play.

On returning, her tea was on the table. She gobbled it all up, but when her mum asked her if she wanted pudding, the hair on Louisa's neck stood on end. She glanced out at the strawberries in the garden.

Louisa's mother placed some pastry on a plate, but there were no strawberries in the strawberry pie! 'If you don't pick the strawberries you can't expect to eat them!' her mum explained.

Elizabeth Taysom (10)
Nafferton Primary School, Driffield

Train Off The Line

'Where is the train? the station master shouted to the signalman.
Bill Smith, the signalman, replied, 'It's broken down up the line; the breakdown train crew are on their way.'
Mr Brown, the station master said, 'How am I going to get these people to their meeting in the city?'
'They'll have to walk!' laughed Bill.

Mr Brown wasn't happy. The waiting passengers insisted that their meeting was urgent and they had to attend. Mr Brown said he would arrange a coach from the bus depot in place of the train, although travelling to the city by bus was like riding a donkey in the Grand National!

The coach crawled down the street as if it were a turtle. Once the people were on the bus, Mr Brown rang the meeting hall to say that the people would be late. The people got to the meeting in the end and it went very well. The breakdown train came and all was right again.

Joel Westaway (11)
Nafferton Primary School, Driffield

PRISONER!

Mantor reached for another apple. Amraint lay slumped against a tree; his cumbersome armour glistened in the gleaming light. The heat was intolerable; sweat cascaded down their foreheads. Mantor sat down biting into a juicy core; something tapped him on the shoulder. 'Stop it,' he moaned.

'Stop what?' replied Amraint.

'Do you mean this?' cackled a voice from behind them.

They jumped to their feet. An elf stood behind them, its sword raised. Mantor and Amraint ran, the tiny elf ran too. Shafts of lightning shot past the soldiers. One of the bolts struck Mantor. He fell.

Gloom surrounded Mantor as he lay on a cold, stone floor. He was in prison. How could this happen? He grasped for his sword. It wasn't there. He looked at the cell door. At the other side of the closed door, his sword hung teasingly. Mantor groaned.

Something long flew past the slit in the door, then again. It seemed to be a volley of arrows. A familiar face flashed past the bars. 'Amraint, in here,' Mantor shouted. The door flung open.

'Let's get out of here!' cried Amraint. They both ran. Never would they let their guard down again.

Harry Holmes (10)
Nafferton Primary School, Driffield

Basketball Blues

'It's not fair, I never get picked for the team,' moaned Joanne. Joanne turned up for every basketball practise, but never got picked for the school team, whereas on the other hand Louise who never turned up for practise was always on the team. The reason for this was because Louise was tall and could score more easily than Joanne could.

One day Joanne's luck changed. Her team were playing Kilham, the best team in the league, when suddenly it happened. 'Ouch, ouch, ouch!' screamed Louise, she had fallen and hurt her ankle. 'Joanne, take over from me now!' Louise demanded. Joanne wasn't going to let her side down and went on to score the winning goal.

She never missed a game from that day forward, she always played and tried her best. Until one day Louise got bored of it and said, 'It's not fair, I never get picked for the team . . .'

Claire Woodmansey (11)
Nafferton Primary School, Driffield

HIGH HEELS

'Where on earth do you think you're going looking like that?' asked Mum.
'To the school disco,' answered Kim.
'I don't think so,' said Mum, 'those heels are far too high - you'll fall and break your ankle!'
Kim told her mum that she needed to wear high heels so she didn't ruin her long flares. But her mum told her she 'looked like a clown' and told her to change her shoes. 'That's not fair. You treat me like a little baby!' shouted Kim.

Kim's mum thought to herself, then said, 'I think there may be an answer.'
'Right, and what exactly are you planning because I'm not getting changed. I saved up all my pocket money for those trousers,' Kim told her mum.
'Don't be so cheeky, otherwise I won't help!' her mum said, slightly raising her voice.

Kim's mum told her that she could take the trousers up so she could still wear them, but with her favourite trainers instead.
'Thanks Mum,' smiled Kim when she tried on her newly-altered outfit.

Just then, her dad walked through the door and said, 'Where on earth do you think you are going looking like that?'

Laurie Glover (11)
Nafferton Primary School, Driffield

The Monster

That night I was home alone because my mum and dad had gone out for their anniversary.

I was watching a horror movie when I heard a crunch coming from the kitchen. What could it be? I slowly crept into the kitchen. There on the table was a dark, small figure. It jumped off and started to come closer and closer my way. I was shaking. Sweat trickled down my face. I couldn't see where it was now. Suddenly I heard a thump then a creak.

It was going up the stairs. I started to follow it. It was going in my mum and dad's room. It started to go mad, it ran on the bed, over the table, in the hallway, back in the bedroom. I ducked in case it hit me, but it didn't.

Then it jumped on the bed, so I switched the light on. It was my rabbit Molly. It must have escaped.

Later, my mum and dad got home and I told them all about it. They started to laugh, but I didn't think it was very funny. Finally, after a cup of hot chocolate and some biscuits I was so tired I went to bed.

Francesca Seetal (10)
St Vincent's RC Primary School, Hull

JULIA

Over 5 million years ago, there lived two Gods, Athene and Elissio Bolgero. They both loved Julia, a goddess, they would do anything for her. Sadly Julia went missing, they couldn't find her anywhere. 'I'll look for her,' cried Ellisio.
'No! I will,' shouted Athene.
'You both will,' exclaimed Zeus.

So off they went. Ellisio came across a massive rock and wondered, how am I going to get along here?
'You will fly,' said a mysterious voice. Suddenly Ellisio started to drift up in the air.

Athene came across five chopping swords. 'How am I going to get along here?'
'You will run,' said a mysterious voice. There and then he was running as fast as a speeding bullet.

They both met at the point where Julia was, but she was guarded by a three-headed monster. 'How are we meant to get past that?' Ellisio said with a thinking look on his face.
'Look, there is a mask over there, we'll scare him,' said Athene. They got the mask and scared him half to death.

'Julia, you're alright,' said Ellisio sorrowfully.
'We found her,' said Athene. So they all had a massive party.

Ellis Todd (9)
St Vincent's RC Primary School, Hull

PHOENIX

I was dragging my feet along the ground on a day as hot as blazes in the sunlight. It was as if the sun had been moved closer to the Earth. Then I realised it wasn't the sun, it was a Phoenix! A beautiful, fiery Phoenix. The Phoenix was trying to lead me somewhere, so I followed it.

The Phoenix led me like a shepherd and his sheep to somewhere I was very scared of, a volcano! Then before I knew it I was slipping off the steep edge of a fiery volcano! I fell, I screamed sharply as I fell towards the lava. 'Help me somebody! But it was no use. Suddenly something grabbed me. It was the Phoenix!

The Phoenix dropped me outside a weird, old lady's house. She explained that this was her super, special robot Phoenix. She'd made quite a few of them. I was so surprised I nearly fell over. In the end I went to my nice, cosy home. When I got home I was just glad that I had been in an adventure with a robot Phoenix.

James Wilson (10)
St Vincent's RC Primary School, Hull

THE HAUNTED CASTLE

Tim was walking up the street when some leaves blew in his face and as if by magic a castle appeared. He was shocked, but he went in. When he got in the castle all that he saw was cracked paintings, massive cobwebs and a dusty stair. Tim approached the stairs and climbed up.

When he got to the top all there was were paintings on the walls. He saw some moving eyes in a painting. Tim moved to the other side of the wall. He fell through. It was a trapdoor.

He held the torch at the eyes. They vanished. He turned around then he got tapped on the shoulder, he turned round again. The eyes were back again. He pushed against the wall, the wall moved. Tim ran for his life down the stairs, through the corridor and outside, he shouted, 'I'm free.'

Tim was running home so fast his feet didn't even touch the ground. Then the building collapsed behind him.

Thomas Salisbury (10)
St Vincent's RC Primary School, Hull

Lost

I will never forget that fateful night. It changed the course of my entire life. I know what I'll do, I'll tell you about it. Then you can see for yourself.

The night was grey. Owls were hooting diligently. A storm was brewing. I was a fool to be walking that late and alone. I thought I saw something moving in the shadows. 'It's nothing,' I said to myself. I walked on. There it was again, by the wall. 'It's nothing,' I said again, breathing heavily.

Suddenly, thunder and lightning started brawling in the sky, leaving a trail of yellow sparks, scattering like spray. I took shelter under a nearby tree. *Crash!* It fell to the floor. Now pink mist was swarming around me.

'Ahhhhhhhhhh!' I screamed. I couldn't believe my eyes. It was the thing I'd seen in the shadows, huge, green and disgustingly hideous. Suddenly, before I had any time to think, it spat this slimy, viscose fluid at me. *Slump!* I fell to the floor. I was paralysed.

It picked me up in its claws and carried me into the mist. I was lost in the clutches of the beast. Forever. Lost.

Rónan James Burns (10)
St Vincent's RC Primary School, Hull

A Living Nightmare

A deathly silence filled the night air. Stormy clouds raced through the sky. Thunder rolled and lightning lashed down like Satan's whip. Lee sat trembling, jumping at every noise or movement. He couldn't sleep. There was something in the house, something watching him, but he didn't know what.

The clock chimed twelve. Lee had finally fallen into an uneasy sleep. His dreams were of graveyards and monsters. He groaned and turned over. Somewhere, deep in the heart of the house something awoke. Its eyes glowed red. It rose up and stumbled to Lee's room.

Like a mouse on silk it crept upstairs. With a bony finger it picked the lock. Silently it crept over to the boy's bed. His uneasy sleep was disturbed. Something was there. Something that had just stroked a claw-like finger over his face. His heart stopped. His eyes flickered open and he saw his worst nightmare. Petrified, he stuttered, 'Whhhat do you want?'
Menacingly, it pointed straight at him and murmured, 'You.'

Suddenly a rush of adrenaline washed over Lee and he sprang out of bed, running for his dear life. Through the winding corridors he ran, constantly looking over his shoulder. Finally he was cornered.

The spirit flew straight into his heart. Lee fell to his knees, clutching at his chest. He was now a tool. His mind and soul were no longer his own. He was nothing.

Emily Rowson (10)
St Vincent's RC Primary School, Hull

THE SKELETON

It was a dark and creepy night. I was in the car on the way to this spooky house, and it was spooky. We were there. I unpacked my things with great difficulty.

I was walking down the corridor when I saw . . . 'It's a zombie . . . no, it's a skeleton,' I said. Then I started hitting myself on the head, this made him laugh.

He laughed so much he lost his head, literally. Then he grabbed his scythe, still with no head and tried to slash me with it. Instead, it got stuck in the floor like a spear in a deer. I pulled it out, there was a big hole.

'Give me the head,' I said to my bother of a brother. He did it. I grabbed the head and threw it down the rubbish chute. The skeleton went down too. I heard the rumble of bones.

While we were leaving, I saw a car pulling in. I knew what was in store for them.

Robert Murray (10)
St Vincent's RC Primary School, Hull

When The Doorbell Rang

I was sitting in my favourite chair watching TV. My mum was out for the week because she was in India and my dad was at a meeting. He said he wouldn't be home till late.

The phone rang. It was my mum. I was so happy because she said she was coming home early. I put the phone down, and I turned the TV over. The police were on. They were on about a man on the run. They said he was a killer.

The doorbell rang. I turned the TV off. My heart was pounding, nearly coming out of my chest. I was scared. Sweat was dropping from my hands. I was frightened. Slowly, I stood up and walked into the hall, the doorbell rang again.

I walked to the door as slow as a tortoise. I grabbed the keys. They trembled in my hands. I opened the door. It was my grandma. I let her come in and join me for a cup of tea.

'I'll never ever, ever watch that programme again.' So I did as I said I would, I didn't watch that programme again. I hope I don't bump into that runaway killer though.

Becky Anholm (9)
St Vincent's RC Primary School, Hull

THE NEVER-ENDING MAZE

It was a nightmare. Mum, my sister and I were going to the never-ending maze. I suspected it was called that because once you were in you were trapped.

My mum kept saying how easy it would be. We approached the thorny labyrinth cautiously. It didn't look too bad, but still I didn't know what lay ahead. Everything was going fine until I took a wrong turning. No problem I thought to myself. I'll just retrace my steps. There *was* just one small problem. The others were nowhere in sight!

Lost! In the never-ending maze. I started biting my nails frantically. I could hear faint murmurs in the distance. Footsteps pounding on the brown, flaky floor. There was crunching behind me. I ran like a bullet. It was hopeless, the person or thing was catching up to me. I collapsed like a pancake on a frying pan. The thing was drawing nearer, I could see its shadow.

'Peter?' that voice sounded familiar. I peered round the corner. My sister! She ran to me.
'How on earth did you get lost?' she gasped.
'The maze *is* complicated,' I replied frozen with shock.

She dragged me round the nearest corner. The look of pleasure on her face was tremendous when she saw I was only a few metres from where I started.

Laurence Harwood (10)
St Vincent's RC Primary School, Hull

A Day In The Life Of James Wilson

My best friend, named James, seems like a normal child, but when he gets to school he will just amaze you. In the morning as soon as he is ready, he will fly to his car and be driven to school.

Once the bell has rung he is very excited for his first lesson, since it's his favourite subject, maths. The teacher gives them a task, the books are given out and James sets to work. He will finish a maths task as if he was an unbeatable mathematician.

At 12 o'clock the bell rings. James dashes outside and decides to play football. His favourite lunchtime game. His tummy does a little rumble, he hopes that he will be eating soon. Suddenly the whistle blows, followed by a scream, '5 and 6 pack-ups.' James' heart is full of joy; he sprints to the dining hall and eats a magnificent lunch. Now it's science, James is working hard and finishes in time.

The sun is going down and now he has to go to the music centre. There he will sing to a beautiful tune. Afterwards he has his tea, climbs into bed and dreams of a planet named 'Maths'.

Liam Carpenter-Robson (10)
St Vincent's RC Primary School, Hull

The Horrible Ghost

Once upon a time there was a horrible ghost that went round everywhere. The ghost went to people's houses and stole everything they owned. Then one night the ghost was out haunting when the stars came up, there he saw a boy walking down the road. The horrible ghost sneaked up to the boy then he grabbed him and floated away.

The ghost went to his secret house where no one could find the boy. The ghost cried out with laughter that he had caught all the children. The children were screaming as the ghost went to look for some more children. He went back to the people's houses, and found three children in bed. I'll get them, I'll take them, he thought.

The ghost took the three children and went away. He went to his house, he now had 100 children there. Then the ghost said, 'I am the best ghost in the world. A worthy winner.'

The ghost thought for one minute then he came up with an idea, as he heard the children cry. He said, 'I shouldn't have taken these children, they need their parents.' The ghost took the children home.

Thomas Trewhitt (10)
St Vincent's RC Primary School, Hull

RATS

All my life I have been scared of rats, just because of one holiday. Let me tell you how I became afraid.

It all started a while back, I was on the way to Whitby in my car. My sister told me that a really, scary pirate lived there. His name was Popeye. We drove by a real scary figure, it just looked like a cloak with a pipe sticking out the end. We were heading towards the Eagle's Eye pub. Then, guess what, the same odd figure was staying at the same pub that we were.

I had my supper and I was heading upstairs then suddenly the scary figure cornered me. He took out the Daily Mail. My heart suddenly stopped beating. Step by step the scary figure drew closer. I looked up and saw an air vent.

I didn't waste the opportunity. I jumped onto the cupboard and punched the air vent. As I was crawling through the vents, I looked up and to my horror there was an infestation of rats. I held my breath as I crawled through them. Suddenly, a giant rat started chasing me. There was a wet patch and I slipped into loads of rats. They all started biting me. Then I spotted an opening and shot right to it.

Later I managed to get back to my bedroom and I could not wait to get to sleep. I was glad that we could leave this place. Now you know why I have a fear of rats.

Charlie Haite (10)
St Vincent's RC Primary School, Hull

A Day In The Life Of David Beckham

I will always remember that goal against Greece. That goal got us to the World Cup finals. Teddy Sheringham asked if he could take the free kick, but I said no. As I was running to the ball, tension grew inside me. I placed my foot in the right position and kicked it. I watched the ball fly in the air. '*Goal!*' someone said. Relief ran through the crowd.

That was then, this is now.

'Whaa, whaa,' Brooklyn was crying. I can't get to him with my broken toe. Later Victoria was making tuna sandwiches. After I ate mine I watched England under 21s play. They beat Switzerland 2-1. I sat down and had a sleep. Meanwhile Brooklyn was playing with my mobile.

It was 4 o'clock. I played on my PlayStation 2 on FIFA 2002. After that it was time for bed. Every step seemed to make my toe worse. Five more metres to Brooklyn's room. When I was in Brooklyn's room I fell asleep about five hundred times. Eventually, I fell asleep, but Brooklyn jumped on me and fell asleep. It has been quite an interesting day for Brooklyn.

Callum McLeod (10)
St Vincent's RC Primary School, Hull

THE SPOOK

One horrible, stormy night a girl called Diz went in the attic. She looked for a game and she found one called *See*. Then she said to herself, 'What game is that?'

She opened the game and found a board and a glass ball. Nothing happened, well it didn't look good anyway. Diz got some milk and then saw a face in the ball.

The eyes were red like fire, her hair was white and knotted like barbed wire. She picked it up to look at it closer, then it burnt her hand. 'Ouch,' she said.
At that moment, Diz dropped it and the face was gone. She put it back in the box.

In the night she looked at the box, then the ball flew in the air. She said, 'Leave me alone,' and the ball dropped to the floor.

The next day she got the box and tied it up in chains, put a lock on it and put it in the attic and did the same to the attic door. From then on everything was alright and there were no more strange things happening.

Sean Anholm (9)
St Vincent's RC Primary School, Hull

A Day In The Life Of My Best Friend

Stephanie Fish is my very best friend and this is how I think her life goes:

Every night a shocking frost creeps across the beautiful, crystal clear sky, but we don't mind the cold. The only problem is I think Stephanie does. It's like she would do almost anything to keep our friendship really strong, like a chain, that's why I like her.

Sorry, sorry, sorry, that's all she ever says. What I mean is, she tries to pretend that I am not bossing her around. I think that I might be.

Stephanie is the best friend that I could ever ask for and I will never let that thought escape my mind. She is crowded, not by people, but by pressure. I just don't want to push the pressure against her. I bet she feels like she's never done anything she's wanted to do before.

All I know is that she loves and cares for me and I do the same. I don't know how she feels, but I feel very lucky to be her best friend. Whenever I'm down she'll cheer me up, she does hard work and succeeds.

I never thought that I'd be this happy. Ever.

Nancy Hawksworth (9)
St Vincent's RC Primary School, Hull

A Day In The Life Of A Hamster

One sunny morning I was in a hamster cage in the pet shop with some other hamsters. A family came in the shop and looked at us, the hamsters. They liked me, a brown and white hamster. Even better, they were going to buy me.

When we got home they named me, they called me Beauty. I loved my cage, it was a three-storey house. My family brought me a little plastic house for my cage. I loved my new home, it was brilliant. I'm glad they bought me.

They fed me every day and checked to see if I was OK all the time. I was really tired so I went to bed, it was very late at night. Suddenly there was a fierce, loud noise coming from near my cage. I got up to go and see what it was. Slowly I crept down the stairs and saw a horrid, ugly rat. He opened the flap on the cage and suddenly he started fighting. The cage fell over with a big bang. My owners came running down the stairs. They checked if I was alright. In the morning they took me to see the vet.

That rat sure deserved what I gave him, a black eye. After that we all got on together.

Stephanie Fish (10)
St Vincent's RC Primary School, Hull

A Day In The Life Of Tim Tiger

A usual day, Tim tiger was rolling in the snow in Siberia playing, when he got on his front he shook his head because he had snow on his nose. Just a second he thought, that's the poachers - because he had heard a gunshot. *Pow!* If I don't hide I will be dead. I've got to find somewhere to hide.

'There he is, get him.'
Tim ran as fast as he could. *Pow!* Missed, nah hah!
Pow! Ahhh! 'Nearly' This time Tim was running faster than ever and he jumped off a waterfall onto land. He saw his friend Beaky. 'Not right now,' Tim spluttered and banged his head on an overhanging branch.
'Ow,' he groaned.
He jumped over a branch (of course you would think it's beginning to be a really wild tiger chase).

Go, go, go. This way, he turned left, then right. He jumped over a monkey, an elephant and a heap of snow. He stopped for breath. He heard a wind, it ruffled his fur. He ran further. He was still tired and ran more. He needed water. He ran and fell into some snow.

Alistair Bromyard (8)
St Vincent's RC Primary School, Hull

Dogs Are Back In Town

Hello, I'm a dog. I don't have a name, I'm a stray, if you haven't guessed. I'll just be a second. *Ruff! Ruff!* I ran after a cat, but something bad came from it. I got caught by the dog pound. I was in luck, because I got fed leftovers from dinner.

One week later an old man came into the pound looking for a dog. He looked at me in a strange way. The old man said I was perfect. I was very chuffed. I heard his whisper, I looked tasty. I thought we were going home, but I wasn't. We were going somewhere called the airport. We got on the plane.

A day later we were in China! I went out to explore, but a fat, hungry China man chased me. I bit him, but he shot me in the leg. A couple of tourists found me and we went back to England and I got taken to the vet.

Leon Martin (9)
St Vincent's RC Primary School, Hull

THE HOODED GHOST

'Os! Os! Our baby!' Ico screeched. Os ran to her in excitement.
'What shall we call him?' wondered Os.
'Numus,' Ico said softly.

Twelve years later Ico walked up to Numus. 'Numus, the day before you were born we had murdered someone called Timos, because he was a mischief maker and he's back. You're the only elf who can kill him and you must! He's weak, he lives off us. Here's your sword.'

Numus ran through the crops, over the bridge and ran into an elf. 'Erm, erm, hello sir.' He turned round his skeleton face, raised his hand at an owl and a zap came out of his hand. The owl enlarged to a giant monster! The monster raised his wing to slap poor Numus who raised his sword and *slash!*
Squack, the monster jumped at him with its beak, *snap!* He just missed him, *'Forccsce!'* The monster turned back into an ordinary owl again.

Numus turned and there in front of him was Timos. Numus raised his sword and it went straight through him! 'Young child this is for you.' He jumped on top of him. Numus was choking, he grabbed Timos's bony face and threw him. He broke and that was the end of him.

Christopher Hopkin (9)
St Vincent's RC Primary School, Hull

Day Of The Murder

Crash! The old lab just imploded.
'Detective Harry, get over there now!' shouted the constable.
'I'm on my way, sir.'
But when Harry got there, there were two people left. Their names were Peter and John.
'Get an ambulance here now,' said Harry.

Later. 'You wanted me sir?' said Harry.
'Yes, we have had a warning there is going to be a murder. We think he's going to kill Peter,' said the constable.
'Who's he?' said Harry puzzled.
'Red Rum,' boom!
'Get on the case now.'
'OK,' said Harry.

Urrr, went Harry's motorbike on his way to Peter's. When he got there Peter was cowering in his bed. 'What on earth?' said Harry.
'Oh take this,' said Peter shaking.
So Harry opened it and it read, *Red Rum.*
'What does it mean?' questioned Harry.
'I don't know,' whispered Peter.
Smash! A rock fell through the window.
'Excuse me,' said Harry and he jumped on his hog and followed the car that was speeding down the road.

Later the car stopped dead in some woods. Harry got off his hog and went into the woods. The only words John said were, 'Red Rum,' and he said them fast.
But Harry shouted, 'The building.'
So they jumped on the building.
'Die,' John said eyeing him. He jumped off the building.
When they got to the bottom he still said, 'Red Rum.'

Oliver Dolphin (9)
St Vincent's RC Primary School, Hull

A GHOST STORY

Right, I'm it and I'm counting to twenty. 'Beth no peeking,' shouted Emma. Emma thought to herself if I hide behind a thick tree maybe Beth won't be able to see me.
'Here I come, ready or not,' Beth yelled.

Beth suddenly heard someone screaming. Beth could tell that it was Emma. She found where Emma was and she had fallen down a wide, muddy hole. Beth was thinking what to do to get Emma out of the hole. Beth said, 'Emma, I've got an idea.'

Beth got a long, old stick. Beth was pulling as hard as she could, but Emma was too heavy. Beth kept on trying to get Emma out, but the stick broke and Beth fell back in.

Then Emma thought that she was sinking and they kept on going down. Just then Emma fell right down to the floor and further. Before Beth fell down she saw a pale-faced man and he saw her, but he just walked straight past her then she fell down too.

They thought that they had fallen into a castle and Beth saw the same pale-faced person. It was a ghost and he whispered, 'Hi, I'm rosseforP erodelbmuD . . .'
'Help!'

Elena Prosser (9)
St Vincent's RC Primary School, Hull

GHOST HOUSE

'Ooh,' the door creaked as it opened. Beth, who was ten years old went walking into a haunted house. But she didn't know this was a haunted house. When she got inside she saw that all the tables and chairs were covered in cloth and cobwebs.

Beth heard drops of water and started to shiver with fear. Beth went walking in the house, she found a toilet. She just had a little peep inside. But it wasn't an ordinary bathroom. Oh no, it was a ghost bathroom.

After she had seen it she started to scream. *'Aaaah!'* Beth ran straight to the front door of the house. She heard something coming down the stairs.

It was saying, 'I'm on the first step, I'm on the second step.'
'It was coming to get me,' she said.

After she heard the noise, the thing was on the landing. Phew, thought Beth it's still got another set of stairs to come down. Beth realised that it was a doll. The doll's head was half hanging off and she was still walking down the stairs still saying, 'I'm on the sixth step, I'm on the seventh step.' By this time Beth thought it was creepy. She fled out the door, never to return.

Claire Medina (9)
St Vincent's RC Primary School, Hull

THE NIGHT FOREST

Quite a while ago there were two children called Lucy and Daniel. The two children fancied going on a forest trip at 9pm. So they went to the dark forest. Whilst they were in the forest they heard something, something strange.

Anyway, they kept on walking. Suddenly, they saw some black capes floating. Lucy screamed. Daniel shouted for help, but it didn't work. They tried to fight them off, but they did not succeed. Luckily, the ghosts retreated. The children were near the exit, then the ghosts came back. They tried to fight them off again, but the ghosts fought back.

About a month later they woke up in hospital as perfect as ever. Their Mum and Dad were there smiling happy as you could be. 'Are you OK?'
'Yes,' I said.
So Lucy said, 'Never could be better.'
When they were back at home Lucy and Daniel were watching television. Daniel said, 'I'm never going on a forest trip again. Never! Never again!'

The next day Lucy was at school. Daniel had been sick. Lucy told the teacher and in the afternoon Lucy had to write a report about what they did on the weekends. *'I know . . .'*

Connor Cheesman (9)
St Vincent's RC Primary School, Hull

Lake Adventure

'Boo,' shouted Louise on Saturday morning in the Lake District. Emma and Jean took Pippin around the lake for a morning walk while Louise and Beth made breakfast, bacon and eggs.

After breakfast Emma turned her back for a minute, Pippin was gone!
Emma ran to tell Louse, 'Louise, Louise.'
'What's the problem?' said Louise.
'Pippin has gone missing!'
'What! Please don't tell Beth and her nanna.'
'We have to tell, they won't mind I'm sure.'

While all this was happening, there were two sneaky, green crocodiles gliding on the muddy lake.

Along the road came Claire. 'Oh you didn't know but I think two crocodiles might have taken him.'
'But which one?'

We all went off crying. Louise and Emma got so upset and they were very worried. So much so that they both jumped in and they both swam deeper. Louise and Emma came back up excitedly and told where they had been. Later on Emma said, 'Where's Louise?'

In one flash Louise walked in the door gasping for breath, 'I know where Pippin is!'
My nan said, 'He is my dog and I've had enough!' She went swimming on her own. Louise directed her, they found him. She picked him up to kiss him. But where was Emma?

Beth Mulchinock (9)
St Vincent's RC Primary School, Hull

THE GHOST STORY

One chilly, dark night, six school friends stayed behind at school to tell ghost stories, a teacher got a drink and everyone drank it. There was a open book on the floor and as they drank they shrank inside the book, Tara tried to kick it open but it was too hard.

Then, out of nowhere a wicked man called Doctor Bad stole Amanda away. Ghosts, witches and vampires tried to kill the others but Tara killed them. 'Help, help, ahh!' Doctor Bad was trying to kill Amanda.
'You wicked man!'
'I know!' chuckled Doctor Bad.

Meanwhile, the other friends tried to look for Amanda. There were loads of traps but they found a friendly lion named Leo. He said, 'What are you doing?'
Lydia said, 'We are looking for our friend Amanda, Doctor Bad has taken her.'
'Wait a minute, Doctor Bad, I know where he lives, do you want me to take you there?'
'Yes, please.' everyone shouted.

Leo took them to Doctor Bad's house. Inside was really creepy and scary, they could hear Amanda screaming. 'Come on, let's go.' shouted Lydia. Everyone took weapons and killed Doctor Bad. They untied Amanda and ran to the entrance.

Amanda wanted to get out of the book and the book magically opened. They grew bigger again by touching the lion. They got detention at school the next day but they didn't care, they were safe.

Shaka Cooper (8)
St Vincent's RC Primary School, Hull

HALLOWE'EN

Hallowe'en is drawing closer. In you go socks, not you shorts, Lydia was saying to herself. *La, la, la, la* came the sound of ringing music.
'Shut up,' shouted Mum cheerily.
'Lydia dear, have you packed your pillow?'
Bring came the sound of the dinner bell chiming round the house.

Lydia went downstairs. No! No! Don't close the book now, I'm only the narrator, so where were we, oh yer, Lydia was going downstairs. For tea she was having fish and chips. After tea she got into the car on the motorway. Lydia looked out of the window, a blur of red, yellow and blue went past, it began to rain.

When they got there the adults unpacked while Lydia and Nicole walked outside until they stopped a little girl was crying, 'What's the matter?' asked Nicole, walking towards her.
'I'm a witch and I've lost my mum.'
'What's your name?'
'Shaka.'

Suddenly a loud *bang* came from behind them, 'Give her here, she's mine.'
'No, I'm not.'
'Get away from her!'
'Quick, get your water pistol.' Lydia yelled.

So they squirted her, at last she went. Another *bang* came and they turned around, the witchling shouted, 'Mummy' and they gave each other a big hug.

Lydia Coyle (9)
St Vincent's RC Primary School, Hull

A Day In The Life Of Bumble

Hi, I'm Bumble the guinea pig, I have a black head and bottom with a yellow stripe round my plump middle. I am one and I have a sister called Honey. Now I'm going to tell you what happened to me yesterday.

Well it started when I was dreaming that me and Honey were running free with no cats to bother us. Here comes Dad to put us in the run for a day. Oh no! Cat! Hide! That was close, a cat came.

I must have some green pepper, I've been watching Honey eating for ages. Now we are not talking about food. Oh here I go, I'm dreaming I'm in a field full of yummy grass but then a cold drop fell on my back and woke me from my dream; rain, I went to shelter. It was getting colder so I huddled up to Honey.

Well it must be nearly bedtime because Emma's come out to give us a hug and I like it the way she strokes me under the chin. Oh Honey stop that, anyway Dad's coming to hug you. After that we went back in the hutch for a good night's sleep.

Emma Wilson (9)
St Vincent's RC Primary School, Hull

The Shrinking Machine

'Yes! I've really made it. I've completed the experiment to make an extraordinary machine.' Dad ran downstairs and yelled, 'I've made a shrinking machine, I have to tell someone, bye!'

Ding dong, David walked in and ran to his room when his mum said, 'Don't go in Dad's room,' but David didn't listen.

David walked into Dad's room and banged into the machine. It started making a chuckling noise then it fired at him. He shrunk down to the size of an ant, it was weird. David shouted for help but it didn't work so he ran into the garden and in the long grass he met another ant.
David said, 'Hi,' but the ant just got its long pincers out ready to bite him so he ran back to the house.

David was so frightened he ran into a French horn. He shouted for help just one more time but it was amplified. Mum came running. She just saw the French horn. Mum picked up the horn and put it on the table. Out David dropped.

She quickly rang Dad and asked him to come home to reverse the change. He made some alterations, it worked in reverse and David was back to normal again.

Adam Keech (9)
St Vincent's RC Primary School, Hull

THE FRIGHT

'Ahhh!' screamed Claire. The four girls were running through the spooky, old graveyard, the strong wind howling in their ears.
'Wait a minute,' murmured Louise sounding quite scared, 'where's Claire?'

The gruesome ghosts had kidnapped her.

'Let her go!'
Claire's face burst into a smile. It was Beth. Beth helped Claire to her feet and ran off. But Beth tripped. She could feel blood oozing out of a gash on her forehead. Quickly she ran back to the others. They hurried on, but now it was becoming extremely dark, they couldn't see where they were going. Claire kept tripping over the gravestones, disturbing more ghosts.

'This is a nightmare,' yelled Paige.
'Yeah, it can't get any worse,' shouted Beth. But it did.

A bright light was shining in the distance; quickly they ran towards the light. It was a church. They ran inside and to their great surprise the ghosts didn't follow.

Later that evening Beth realised that Paige was missing.
'She must have been taken by the ghosts,' said Louise.
'Come and see this,' called Claire, it was Paige's hair bobble but next to it was a gravestone with her name on it!

Louise Wilson (9)
St Vincent's RC Primary School, Hull

TRAPPED!

'Come on, we're all ready.' Dave was shouting for Kelvin who was still packing. They were going on holiday to Tenerife.
All of them were sitting in the car when Kelvin said, 'Wait my bag is still inside.'

They set off and halfway to the airport the car suddenly came to a halt.
'What's happened?'
'I'll get out and see,' said Dave.
He opened the car bonnet and looked inside. A rat had made itself a nest. What's this, wondered Dave? It was some wires.

A little distance ahead there was a dusty signpost, half of it was covered up. Louise went to rub the dust off, she found it said *'Little Fields, 5 miles'*. Janet saw the sign. She told Dave that if anyone should go for help it should be her.

Off she went arriving at Little Fields later on. She went to the petrol station. The door was open, Janet stepped in, she found herself looking at a man eating. 'Do you want to join me?' he asked slyly. She didn't say a word. The man inspected her hands. He said, 'They look dirty.' He led her to a room. Next, she found herself on the floor with ghosts all around . . .

Paige Boxshall (9)
St Vincent's RC Primary School, Hull

A Day In The Life Of Charlotte The Millipede

Hi, I'm Charlotte the millipede and welcome to a day in my life.

Well yesterday I was just in the jungle and I saw another millipede in my territory. I was so angry; I wanted to sting her with my pincers. She was wiggling along as if she was so happy she wouldn't care where she was.

It was time to spring when she came up to me and said, 'Hi, my name is Beatrice, do you want to be my friend.' I was gobsmacked.
I'd never been asked to be a friend before. Well maybe that was because I'd never cared about friends before.

I said, 'Yes,' before I could stop myself.
So there we were friends. We decided to go to the Rock Café. We were halfway through our white cocoa cappuccino when we heard shrieking coming from outside. We went to see what was going on. There was a giant cricket stomping all over the shops. The paramedics were there trying to fight the cricket. I counted all the dying millipedes but there were just too many to count. Beatrice and me decided to go home on a cart because it was safer.

When I got in, I went to get my book and read for half an hour. Then I dropped off with my book over my head.

Emily Stout (8)
St Vincent's RC Primary School, Hull

VICKY AND FRIENDS GO TO TOWN

Hi, I'm Victoria but my friends call me Vicky.

Last week the telephone rang and Emily said that Emma, Paige, Louise, Lydia and Claire were going to town tomorrow. So we all met at town, and we went into Claire's Accessories. Just then we saw a man who was strangely dressed with a big hat and a long purple cloak. We all giggled while I was thinking of a plan. I told everyone my plan and then we got into action.

We followed the man to the bakers. I bought an apple pie, I gave my friends a bit but they didn't like it. Then we went into a restaurant (a very posh restaurant) but I tripped over and the pie went into a lady's face. We got chased all the way down the narrow cobbled road and on the way we knocked down some flowers and signs. We got so tired we collapsed and gave up. We all went home and my mum was standing at the door, she knew what had happened so she grounded me for a week.

I'm so bored being locked in my room. I thought I might as well write in my diary. Well gotta go, bye.

Charlotte Lee (9)
St Vincent's RC Primary School, Hull

The Thing

Five minutes until bedtime. Four minutes, three minutes, two minutes, sixty seconds. It struck eight o'clock. After being off school for six weeks I jumped into my bed and rested my head and in about thirty minutes I was asleep.

My dream was just starting! I was in a dark alley and it was cold - like 5°c. My heart was beating fast! In fact very fast. It was pure silence and very dark. I kept on hearing a rustling sound and a screeching sound like a fork rubbing against a plate.

All of a sudden my shoulder dropped and something scratched me on the face and leg! Now my heart was beating a thousand miles an hour. Then something dug into my left leg! I forgot I was dreaming - it was only my cat!

Ryan Ellerby (10)
Scarcroft Primary School, York

Boo!

The air in the town of Marazion was still, clammy and pungent. The 'Old Cornish Pasty' pub, was surprisingly quiet for that time of evening, all that could be heard was a hoarse whisper in the back room.

Two small children stepped out of the door, leading to the back room. Hand in hand, and clutching a paper bag each, they crept to the big oak door, opened it, and slid out.

A figure, dressed in an unbelievable white, had perched him or herself on the bay windows of the pub and was staring straight at the two children.

The figure, now recognised as a woman, slid down to the children. At the first sight of her, the children fled behind the dustbins, 'It's all right,' she said in a low soothing tone, 'I will not harm you, yes, I am a ghost, but all I want is your bags!'
The children timidly handed over the bags, the ghost looked inside, 'Just as I thought, you've been tampered with! Look in the bags, go on look . . .'

'Boo! Happy Hallowe'en!' The two children's brainy godparent had been up to his old Hallowe'en tricks again.

That's the end of Boo!

Molly Crosland (10)
Scarcroft Primary School, York

HALLOWE'EN

It must have been midnight at the time. Everyone should've been asleep by then. But not tonight. For tonight was Hallowe'en night. The last of the trick-or-treaters were left. Just a few teenagers having some fun. One of them was me.

We were walking down one street laughing as we went, when suddenly we noticed the abandoned house. Nobody had lived there for years, but the door was wide open and the noises were so loud. Without thinking we walked straight to it.

Then we saw it. Inside was the foulest thing we'd ever seen. It was tinted green and really slimy and scaly. Its voice boomed out in a bloodcurdling screech saying, 'One of you will be my next victim.'

We all knew what he meant. I was pushed forward. I couldn't believe my friends did that. Fangs sunk into me. Slime covered me. I was gone. Only my clothes were left. But I was still alive, still alive inside the thing's body.

Eleanor Rushton (9)
Scarcroft Primary School, York

WINTER'S DOMAIN

Winter's icy claw held the crumbling castle. On the bleak hill surrounded by dark, barren land, winter lingered. Snow had long since left the castle's grounds. On the battlements skeletons rotted. A moan rose from the grounds. Outside, facing the gates, a young boy shivered.

Down in the town Summer's face was smiling. People could see the castle. They couldn't see the boy. No, nobody could see Jonmettie. The market bustled and crowded. Nobody knew how long the castle had been there. Nobody knew its secret.

Jonmettie pushed open the gate, over his head bats flew out. In front of him stone walls echoed the sound of the gates closing. In front of him stood a man. He was so pale and seemed semi-translucent. He turned and walked through Jonmettie, who felt as if a ton of ice had fallen on his head. It was a ghost.

In the town Winter was feared. Jonmettie ran, straight through a door. into a large chamber in which a creature laughed. 'I am Winter.' it cackled. 'So Jonmettie, come to battle?' A claw flashed out. Jonmettie was in Winter's domain.

Jonathan Burr (10)
Scarcroft Primary School, York

THE HOUSE OF DEATH

Creak . . . the door opened before he even knocked. A chill swept through Josh. 'Freaky' said his heart.
'So what?' said his brain. He wandered in, the door slammed behind him.

He started to tiptoe round, searching for the gem. He found it inside a Venus flytrap. There was a long corridor to the right of Josh, he crawled through, as the ceiling was so low, all the doors were locked and they all had strange patterns on them.

At the end of the long corridor Josh stopped for a rest. he could hear footsteps behind him. He ran, how he ran, up the stairs and into a hall covered in cobwebs. The footsteps died out.

Josh looked round him, according to the instructions given by the wizard at the beginning, the next gem was in there. This time it was inside a strange looking wine glass.

Josh looked down, he was standing on . . . nothing! Down, down, down he fell.

'Game over,' said the PC!

Fred Woodcock (9)
Scarcroft Primary School, York

A Day In The Life Of A Class Hamster

Every hamster has a name and it's the same with the class hamster.

I am called Peanuts and this was a day in my life. As usual I woke at a quite early time (I may be clever but I can't tell the time) when I got out of bed I walked around looking for food. I had my breakfast and then went climbing. The teacher wasn't here yet so I hid in my bed and talked to Bramble (another hamster) on my secret telephone. He told me that when they got me out I could run away. I didn't want to run away but this did give me an idea . . .

When the children came in the class I noticed they were wearing trousers. These must be boys I thought. Two of them played with me. Their trousers had wide legs on them, I could easily get up there and hide. Then I could get home with him and see Bramble. Bramble belongs to him!

The boys got up to go. I fell out with a bump! When the boy saw me he laughed very loudly and put me back. No more escaping for me! For now anyway!

Daniel Lemmon (9)
Snaith Primary School, Nr Goole

THE MAGIC HAT

There was once a lonely middle-aged man called Ben. He was running low on money so he sold his black and pointed hat at the market.

Ben sold his pretend magic hat for £25 to a rich man. The next day the rich man came and knocked loudly on Ben's cottage door. The man at the door looked as if he was going to burst at any second. 'I want my money back.' he roared at Ben. Ben's smile was soon wiped of his grinning face. 'If you don't give it back then I will . . .' he looked thoughtfully, then nodded his head.

Ben hurried into his cottage, up to his room, under a floorboard and got the sack from under the bed, then walked slowly down the stairs carefully holding the sack of money.

Just before Ben handed the money over he asked, 'What would you have done if I had not returned your money?'
'Well' he replied thoughtfully, ' I would have just had to earn more money.' With that he smiled and walked away.

Marie Moles (10)
Snaith Primary School, Nr Goole

The Magic Hat

One day Mr Tanton was bored! He had nothing to do. He sat and watched TV. On Channel One was the news. The news reporter said there was a one of a kind magic hat, which was worth *millions.* Mr Tanton had a top hat that looked just like the one that he saw on TV. Therefore, he decided to sell it. He put it for sale at £5,000!

Mr Megginson came along and decided to buy it. As soon as Mr Megginson had walked away, Mr Tanton rushed off to Cyprus. When Mr Megginson got home and noticed it was a fake, he tried to contact him. However his answer machine said, 'I'm sorry but Mr Tanton is not here right now, please leave a message after the beep.'

He decided to sue him. Nevertheless, not even the professionals could track him down. So Mr Megginson said, 'If you can't find him then I'll find him.' As he walked away, he thought how am I going to do this?

Mr Megginson hadn't noticed Mr Tanton's next-door neighbour, Mr Ohikary, was out trimming his hedge. 'How am I going to do this?' groaned Mr Megginson.
In addition, to this surprise Mr Ohikary said, 'It's quiet now Mr Tanton's gone to Cyprus.'
'Cyprus!'
'Yes Cyprus.'
'Whereabouts?'
'To Nicosia, he's just left!'

Therefore he flew to Cyprus and to his surprise Mr Tanton was sitting there. Mr Megginson said, 'Give me back my money or I'll . . .'
'OK, here, take it!'
'Thank you.'
'Tell me, what would you have done?'
'Nothing really!'

Jacob Puckering (9)
Snaith Primary School, Nr Goole

A Day In The Life Of Jack The Greyhound

Jack is a family pet who can get into lots of trouble.

Hi! My name is Jack and I am very lazy. My owner is called Sophie and she is very kind. Sometimes she even sneaks some of her dinner to me.

But guess what? Today I got really told off just because I knocked gravy over so I ran away. I ran into the graveyard but the vicar saw me and took me home.

The next night when all was quiet I ran like mad out of the open back door. I managed to get out of the gate. I saw Claire, Sophie's best friend. I ran up behind her and followed her all the way to Oakdale Close where Claire lives.

The next morning she found me in her bedroom and took me home. Sophie was very upset and never ever let me out of her sight again.

Sophie Gardner (10)
Snaith Primary School, Nr Goole

THE STRANGE MIRROR

Tom and Harriet had just moved house. This house was no ordinary house. Many strange things happened at night. At the bottom of the stairs was a mirror, a gold mirror that the people before had left.

The next night Harriet was combing her hair in the mirror when she heard a drip noise, like it was from a tap. Then red water started to fall from the ceiling. This made Harriet run to her mum as quick as lightning. She explained to her mum what had just happened. Harriet's mum walked over to the mirror scared and shocked. Her mum couldn't see anything. Harriet felt quite stupid and her mum told her to go to bed.

But the next morning when her mum was putting on her make-up, the blood started to drip from the ceiling onto the mirror in front of her. Then it started to happen to all the family. Everyone was scared to go to bed. So, through the night the family started to pack their suitcases. At 1am the family ran to a hotel. They checked in and went to their room. None of them could get a decent night's sleep.

And from then on the family began looking for a new home.

Sarah McGuinness (10)
Snaith Primary School, Nr Goole

The Glowing Coin

There was once a boy who lived in a small village called Hallington with his mum, dad and sisters. His name was Harry. He lived in a small house at the bottom of an alley.

One day he was coming home from school when he found a coin on the floor. He picked it up and took it home, had his tea and told his mum all about what he found and what he did. When he went to bed he couldn't get to sleep. He was thinking about the coin all the time.

Eventually he got to sleep but suddenly woke up and heard a strange noise. The coin that he found was glowing and spinning around. He picked it up and started to get smaller and smaller and then eventually got sucked in.

After ten minutes he realised where he was. He was gobsmacked. He was in his sister's doll house. He heard a loud bang on the door and saw a large figure come through. He looked like a wrestler! It was The Rock Harry picked up a 20p and chucked it at The Rock's head.
The head came off and he shouted, 'Can you spell 'hello' in Latin?'

He found the coin back in his pocket and suddenly he found himself back in his room.

Jack Wilson (10)
Snaith Primary School, Nr Goole

A Day In The Life Of Rafaella

8.30am	I left for school. Everyone I passed whispered 'Earwig' or 'Wiggy'.
8.50	I arrived at school. Lucy bugged me by trying to apologise. I shook her off.
8.55	The boys all chorused 'Earwig' as I entered the classroom. Miss was not there (luckily for the boys).
9.00	Miss Clabbert arrived and caught Jordan passing me a note reading 'Wearing new wigs today, Big Ears?'
9.43	Miss told me off for not taking heed in maths.
10.11	We were allowed out to break early. Lucy started bugging me again.
10.30	I trudged back to the classroom unhappily, ready to be bored asleep by literacy. (Literacy was boring so I won't tell you about it)
12.00pm	We flowed into the dining hall and I ate my sandwiches miserably. I spent a lonely play time afterwards.
1.30	As we headed back to class, I saw Lucy looking sad, like me. Luckily we were doing art, my favourite subject, so I cheered up a bit.
2.01	Our deputy head interrupted as we started for the music room. I caught 'no instruments'. No music? Huh! We did it in the classroom. I received a note saying 'Ear-wi-go! Ear-wi-go! Ear-wi-go!'
2.30	We went to break and Lucy asked me to be friends. Again! For some reason I said, 'Yes!' and blushed. We said, 'Sorry' together and giggled. Brad came running up shouting 'Ear-wi-go!' but I was happy. I had found a new friend.

2.45 The bell rang and me and Lucy made our way to class, when Lucy blurted out with 'Doawannacumtomashows?' and went red. 'Sorry! Do you want to come to my house?' 'Ooh! Yes please!' I replied, 'I'll ask my mum.'

3.30 I asked my mum as we exited school. Her response was an obvious, 'Yes' so I can safely bring today's dairy to an end.

Nicholas Moore (9)
Snaith Primary School, Nr Goole

A Day In The Life Of Bard

I could see the hope of the dragon. It was to burn our entire town. But I did not care if I had to sacrifice my life to kill him.

All my arrows gone, but then I spotted my last one, my black arrow. I was getting it ready to shoot when something swooped to my shoulder. It startled me half to death. But it was only an old thrush, but because I was from the race of Dale, I could understand it's language.

Its words were, 'Wait, look for the hollow in the left breast, try as hard as you can to shoot it there!'

So I stretched the bow then struck, it all fell silent, it hit him right in the heart! The dragon was killed! As it fell down, cheering filled the island, then the splash from his falling cleared all the fire from sight! I was a hero!

Emily Carey (9)
Snaith Primary School, Nr Goole

A Day In The Life Of Rafaella

It was play time and Rafaella was sat in the corner of the playground fiddling about with some very small stones. Lucy was searching for Rafaella. 'Rafaella! Where are you?' called Lucy with a loud high-pitched voice.
'Ah, there you are' mumbled Lucy. 'I've just come to apologise about what happened earlier.'

Rafaella ignored her and looked down at the floor with her arms folded. Lucy frowned and said, 'Did you hear me . . . I'm sorry.'
Rafaella looked up and stared at her. 'No, I'm not going to be your friend, everyone's calling Earwig now and it's all your fault,' bellowed Rafaella. Lucy said nothing and walked away.

When it was time to go into class Lucy talked to her teacher about what had just happened. The teacher said, 'Rafaella, please come and see me after class . . . you too Lucy.'

Class finished, Lucy and Rafaella stayed behind.
'So girls, I'm sure everyone will be happier if we all become friends and treat each other kindly,' said the teacher smiling.
Lucy turned to Rafaella, 'So will you be my friend now then?'
'No, I'll be your best friend,' said Rafaella with a smile. And that was the beginning of a new friendship.

Hannah Bartle (9)
Snaith Primary School, Nr Goole

ALIENS IN THE YEAR 2002

It was the year 2002
'Cwash landing!' shouted chief alien of the Star Traveller.
'Oof! Ow! Yeeow!' Meanwhile, people on Earth see the Star Traveller, they think it's a tornado.
'Batten down the hatches! It's a twister!' called the watchers.

Back in the spaceship, second alien in command looked out of the window and said, 'We're spinning so fast, can't see a thing! Wadoof!'
'We've landed.' said the chief.

'Hey! That was no tornado, it was a spaceship spinning 333333.3319mph' said one of the watchers. Suddenly, they heard a clanking noise and some strange looking aliens stepped out.
'This unknown planet looks . . . strange.' said one alien.
'So do they!' said another and pointed to the watchers.

'We come in peace,' said one of the watchers. They all shook hands.
'What are your names?' asked another watcher.
'Zilch,' said one.
'Zin,' said another.
'Zoink,' said the next in the line.
'Zink,' said the last one.
'What awe youws?'
'Bill, Bob, Sally and Boris.'
'The west of the cwew awe inside, come in,' said Zilch.

The spaceship only had one room, but a fascinating room it was. It had computers and food storers but they went straight to the chief!

Jonathan Crossley (8)
Snaith Primary School, Nr Goole

All The Ice Cream In The World

'Hi, I'm Jay, I'm the hero of this story.'
'Hey, who are you calling Hero, I was the one who knocked out the goblins and you only did all that work to save your favourite ice cream, chocolate munch.'
'OK, OK, let's just get on with the story, that annoying pixie is my friend.

It all started a month ago, when this madman was going to destroy all the ice cream in the world and keep all the ice cream factory people as slaves.

Well this madman was called Dr I C Destroyer and he had two twerps of bodyguards, Bert and Kirk. So me and my pixie were just walking along or in my pixie's case, gliding, then out of the blue two goblins came and grabbed us, of course I put up a tremendous fight.'

'You didn't put up a fight, you were too busy making sure your hair wasn't messy!'

'But they managed to pull us down a hole, I tripped over a lot. Soon we got there to a giant tub of ice cream and a tube of boiling water, it was about to open when at the speed of light my pixie picked up the troll's clubs, bashed the trolls on the head and whacked Dr I C Destroyer into the tube and blocked it.

The police came and instead of arresting the mad doctor they gave him a job, his worst nightmare, he became an ice cream man.'

Edward Coulden (8)
Snaith Primary School, Nr Goole

The Vampire's Revenge

1,000 years ago a vampire was sent to his coffin, for sucking the blood from a million people. But he has now escaped.

Tom went to the Stone Age castle. He walked in, something tapped him on the shoulder, he froze, turned around, there in front of him was the vampire. He opened his mouth but no sound came out. He ran for his life, the doors shut, he was trapped. The vampire came nearer, he put his fangs near Tom's neck. Tom pushed the vampire into the coffin, he was gone.

When Tom got home he told his mum and dad, they told him about the legend. The next morning he was in the newspapers, TV and radio, he was a hero!

One year later Tom went back to the castle, he did not feel scared. The air felt cold, his hands went numb, he thought his nails would come off. The door blew open, a dark figure walked in, Tom knew who it was, it was the vampire, his fangs were shiny. 'Hello, my dear friend, sorry I scared you, I was just getting up!' he said.
'I thought you had gone!' said Tom, pulling out a clove of garlic. The vampire fell to the floor begging for mercy.
'Please no!'
'Oh yes!' said Tom. Then the vampire was dead.
'No more bloodsucking for this vampire!' said Tom.

Jasmine Wright (8)
Snaith Primary School, Nr Goole

HAZEL THE WITCH AND THE MISSING CAT

Hazel had a cat called Maisy. Hazel was in bed. *Ding, ding!* Her alarm went off, so she got up and dressed. Hazel called Maisy, but Maisy did not come so Hazel went to Maisy's basket but he was not there. This is a mission for Hazel!

Hazel got on her broomstick and zoomed off in the sky. She was looking high and low, then she saw her best friend Tony. 'Hi,' said Tony, 'what are you looking for?'
'Maisy!' said Hazel.
Tony said, 'I shall help you.'

So Tony and Hazel were on their brooms looking for Maisy. They were zooming across the bewitched lands when they saw Jimmy. 'Hi,' said Jimmy, 'what are you looking for?'
'Maisy!' said Tony and Hazel.
'I shall come and help you,' said Jimmy.

So Jimmy, Tony and Hazel went up in the sky, then Tony saw Jasmine and Jessica. 'What are you doing?'
'Looking for Maisy!'
'We shall come and help you.'

So Jimmy, Tony, Hazel, Jessica and Jasmine were on their broomsticks.

Then . . . Hazel saw Maisy with Steph. They were both tucking into Steph's delicious home-made pie, Maisy's favourite food. 'Ow, Steph. Thank you.'
'You're welcome.'

So Steph invited Hazel, Maisy, Jasmine, Tony, Jimmy and Jessica for a cup of tea and cake.

Rebecca Watts (8)
Snaith Primary School, Nr Goole

The Man In The Dream

'Arrrgghh' I screamed, then I screamed again, even louder than the last time.
'What is it?' What's the matter Sarah?'
'It's him! Look, it's him!' The tears were now flooding over my night-dress.
'Can't you see? It's him, look!'
'Yes love, calm down. You've had a nightmare, now, come and sleep in my bed tonight.' said Mum, in a reassuring voice.

I woke up a couple of times in the night, but I didn't wake Mum. She needed her sleep.

The next morning, I went out for a bit of fresh air. I stood outside the corner shop, looking at the notices, then a man came out of the shop. I saw a glimmer from a knife or a gun in his pocket. I screamed, then I collapsed.

He was the man from the dream . . . I sat up in the hospital bed, and rolled over. I could see in the dim light that there was a shadow of a man at the end of the ward. The figure was coming nearer to me. His face looked familiar. I screamed . . . *It was him!*

Flora Squire (11)
Snaith Primary School, Nr Goole

Hamsters And Treasure

Once upon a time there were three children who lived in an orphanage, while they waited for their fathers to return from the war in America.

They weren't sisters of course, and weren't related. Their names were Alison, Jackie and Stephanie and Stephanie had a hamster with five baby hamsters.

But one day the hamsters had disappeared so Stephanie went to tell Jackie and Alison. They started looking for Twinkle and her babies. Suddenly Jackie found a door and told Alison and Stephanie.

There were six treasure boxes and so they opened them, only they were empty. The next day the hamsters were back in their cages. It seemed odd because there was treasure in their food bowls.
Alison cried, 'I think this is the treasure from the boxes.'
'I think you may be right.' said Jackie.

The bell rang and Deidre (the orphanage owner) opened the door and three gentlemen were at the door. 'We would like our daughters back,' they said.
Then Alison, Jackie and Stephanie came downstairs and gave their dads the biggest hugs ever and showed them the treasure.

Stephanie Wade (10)
Snaith Primary School, Nr Goole

The Phantom In The Photocopier

'Why won't this blooming photocopier work? Mr Willson's been five times to fix it this week.' Mr Jackson's voice echoed away, the bell rang.

'Hurry up Phil,' said my best friend Billy. Our houses are two and a half miles away from school so we have a long walk home. Suddenly I remembered I had left my homework at school. Billy went to tell my mum while I went to get my homework.

I ran as quick as I could, if I didn't get to school they would lock-up. Finally I reached the doors and shot in, but something stopped me dead in my tracks. It was in the photocopier . . .

Its eyes shone like emeralds. It seemed to be frightened of my appearance and scuttled away revealing black scaly skin. Had I really seen it? My mum was always telling me I had a good imagination. I got my homework and ran home.

The next day everyone (especially Mr Jackson) were surprised as the photocopier was up and running. 'Whatever got into it?' said Mr Jackson, but I knew.

Faye Brignall (10)
Snaith Primary School, Nr Goole

THE MYSTERIOUS PURCHASE

'How much further until we get out of this horrible car?' cried Phil.
'Not long now, we are nearly there,' said Dad.
They turned the next corner and came to a screeching halt. In front of them was a big market, crowded with people.

Phil approached a stall with china dolls on it. 'I would like this one please.' said Phil.
He paid the man, turned and walked away, 'I want it back, I made a mistake,' the man said.
'It's mine now I've bought it,' said Phil. Phil turned and ran to Dad's car.

As Phil got home the phone started to ring. A voice said, 'Give it back, I won't ask you again!'
Phil slammed the phone down.

Phil ran upstairs to his bedroom and on the door read, 'I *will get it back*!' Phil grabbed the doll and ran down to the market stall and said, 'I give in, here have the doll!'
The man gave a chilling smile.
Phil thought to himself, I'll never buy a doll again.

Amy Hardy (11)
Snaith Primary School, Nr Goole

THE SURPRISE EGG

One day Philippa, my best friend came to my house to play. We played and played. Suddenly a parcel arrived. It was an egg that had a tag on which said;

'Happy Easter
Open your egg outside
Love Aunt May xxx'

'Why open it outside?' I said to Philippa.
'I think you'd better, something peculiar might happen!'

On Easter Day, what a sight! Everywhere you looked there were piles and piles of chocolate! I found my pile, I had six Easter eggs. Just then Mum added one to my pile, it was the one from Aunt May. I saved Aunt May's until last, because I thought it might be the best. At last I got to Aunt May's. I grabbed the Easter egg and ran into the back garden.

I ripped off the purple foil. It was a chocolate egg, but then it started to tremble and wobble and shake. I stood back in shock. The egg suddenly cracked open! Silver floating fireworks, *bang, crash, whoosh, whizz, boom!* Everybody came to see what all the noise was about. There everyone stood watching the beautiful scene. 'A firework Easter egg!' said my brother. Everyone laughed out loud!

Kelly Taylor (11)
Snaith Primary School, Nr Goole

The Dark Shadow

Tim looked out of the window with fright and saw a dark shadowy figure in the garden next door which mysteriously kept bending down to pick something up off the plants. Then the dark figure dropped the objects onto the ground and crushed them one by one.

The next day Tim walked into the classroom with a puzzled look on his face. 'What's up Tim?' asked his best friend Joe. Tim told Joe about the night before. Joe wanted to see for himself so he came to stay over at Tim's house that night.

'You know that fishing net that your Dad used to reel that carp in at the pond, has he still got it?'
'Yer, but what do you want with an old fishing net?' replied Tim.
'To catch the dark shadow of course,' said Joe.

Tim ran to get the net and they snuck outside. They flung the net over the shadow's head and brought him to the ground. 'Hey, what do you think you're doing?'
'I'm only killing the snails that are eating my prize plants.' said old Mr Greenfingers from next door as he pulled off the fishing net.

Tim and Joe did feel foolish!

Matthew Smith (10)
Snaith Primary School, Nr Goole

GIRLIE GIRLS, NOT TOMBOYS!

I chucked my mucky tracksuit on. 'Alex!' Mum's voice echoed up the stairs.
'I'm not called Alex, call me Az, I am a tomboy.'

I hurled myself down the small staircase. Then I noticed that the house flooded with people dressed in smart clothes. Suddenly I saw my sister. Josy-Rose, twirling in her puffy wedding dress. 'Oh Alex, go change into your dress, everyone else is ready!'
'Az!' I shouted as I turned and stormed upstairs. I pulled on my white Nike tracksuit.

I sat in the back of the limo with my skateboard beside me. We pulled up outside church. I leaped out of the limo and skated up to the church doors. There, I met Zoz, my best mate, wearing white and blue Reebok clothes. Together we walked in the church, only to see Kelly and Faye in little white bridesmaid dresses starting. We just walked on. People gave me and Zoz funny looks as we went down the aisle.

Suddenly, our mates appeared one by one. All wearing dresses. Little white puffy ones, just like Josy-Rose's! All Girlie girls! *Not* Tomboys!

Lucy Walton (10)
Snaith Primary School, Nr Goole

PROFESSOR JELLYBEAN AND THE TIME MACHINE

'*Eureka*!' shrieked Professor Jellybean, as she leaped into her new motor car. 'Now to test my beautiful invention!' She turned the key and, nothing happened. 'Damn!' she yelled, and kicked the car door. Suddenly a beautiful bright light appeared. Professor Jellybean and the car were gone!

Professor Jellybean woke with a start. She was completely surrounded by a crowd of people all gazing at her, and her car. Just then a shrill whistle sounded, and a number of policemen surrounded the Professor!
'What's all this then!' A gruff sergeant with a handlebar moustache said.

It was only then when she realised that she hadn't created a motorcar, she'd made a time machine, and she was in Victorian times! 'She's a witch!' people screamed.
'She's under arrest!' the sergeant echoed!

The next day, people all around flocked to see her, including Queen Victoria! 'How did you get here?' she snootily exclaimed.
'I . . . I'll show you hen, get me my machine.' The machine was pushed forward. Immediately, she jumped into it, kick started it, and shouted, 'Bye hen!'

The last thing she saw was the magnificent sight of Victoria's bloomers as her dress shot up from the wind of the machine!

Rachael Grimes (10)
Snaith Primary School, Nr Goole

TEDDIES FANTASY WORLD

The doors banged shut. The plump security guard was snoring away. Big teddy looked round cautiously and down came small teddies, big teddies, penguins, dogs, *bang!*

The teddies shot back to their places, quick as lightning, then down below, all those eyes staring down on him. The smallest teddy in the room had banged the drum.

Then all of a sudden, down below, mouths watering, the teddies saw a table laden full of crispy, crunchy biscuits, smooth, spongy cakes, and melted milk chocolate. And then they saw the biggest most magnificent cake in the world.

They couldn't hold out any longer, down, down they plunged. Cakes, buns and biscuits all being grabbed by the teddies. All the Barbie dolls were dancing, keeping everybody entertained. The drunker teddies were playing cards, betting their biscuits.

Suddenly the teddies heard the clank of the cleaning ladies' buckets. They pushed, pulled and scuttled back to their places. Once the cleaning ladies got to the teddy parlour they couldn't understand why there were so many crumbs and a packet of cards lying abandoned on the floor.

So now you know teddies do come alive at night.

Jessica Bridge-Dunk (11)
Snaith Primary School, Nr Goole

Captain Boxer Shorts And The Destructive Doctor Dumpy Diaper

Harold Hutchinson and Fred Filbert are two very clever and sophisticated children (or so their parents say) but obviously they don't know what their children get up to at school.

'Hey, Fred look. Let's change the letters around on that magnetic letter board.'
'Yeah, good idea. Mmmm, I wonder what we can change *why not take a slice of our specially tasty and yummy chocolate pudding today* into?'

A few minutes later . . .

'Ha nice one!' shouted Harold. They'd just changed the letters around had come up with *Mr Casey smells!* Suddenly a massive shadow cast over the two mischievous boys.
'Caught you two red-handed. Get to class.' bellowed Mr Casey (the principal).

'Hello class.' said the new science teacher. 'My name is Doctor Dumpy Diaper.' The class burst out laughing. 'You may laugh now but you won't once I take over the world.'
'This looks like a job for Captain Boxer Shorts!' shouted Fred.
Suddenly Mr Casey stepped into the room.
Click went Harold's fingers and there stood Captain Boxer Shorts. 'What's the problem!' he shouted.
'The Doctor!' everyone replied. Captain Boxer Shorts took out the toilet of truth and blasted the doctor. *'Hooray for Captain Boxer Shorts!'*

Ryan Garbett (10)
Snaith Primary School, Nr Goole

SUPER DRAGON

Faraway in a dark, damp cave lived a dragon. The dragon was called Fire, however he never breathed fire! He lived on the outskirts of a little village in Germany. The people were very scared of Fire but Fire was more scared of them. When Fire went up to them to make friends they all ran home shouting, 'Dragon on the loose!'

Fire's dark, damp cave looked over the beach. One sunny day Fire was admiring the glorious view, of happy children swimming in the sea, also building sandcastles in the sand. He was watching a little girl in the sea, who looked as if she had only just learnt how to swim. He turned round to make a drink when he heard her screaming.

Immediately Fire flew out of his cave, swooped down and scooped her up and landed roughly on the ground. Everyone congratulated him on his outstanding performance.
'Thank you for saving me,' a little voice said. It was the girl, he had saved.

Fire was a hero, he had a palace of his own. He was no longer afraid of humans and humans were no longer afraid of him. He is famous throughout the world.

Megan Flanagan (11)
Snaith Primary School, Nr Goole

Return Of The Werewolf

In the middle of the forest there is a little village. In the village there were four friends, Mathew, Peter, Alex and John.

Over the last few weeks people who lived in the village started to disappear. The four friends decided to go into the woods and investigate.

They each found a weapon incase there was something horrible out there. The next day they set off into the forest. It was very dark in the forest so they needed a torch. They had been walking for a very long time when they found a dead body. They were all very shocked!

They looked up and saw a shadow moving in the trees. They were so mad they all started to chase the shadow. But the shadow turned round on them and started to growl. The next thing they knew the thing had pounced on John and started to eat him.

Mathew, Alex and Peter pulled out their weapons and started to shoot the creature. It fell on the floor *dead!* They were just in time to stop it eating John alive. They pulled him to his feet and carried him back to the village. They all lived happily ever after.

Mathew Hobson (11)
Snaith Primary School, Nr Goole

A Tale Of The Mysterious Book

Do you want to hear a story?

Well, my friend Jessica and I agreed to meet at the bookstall in the market. It was my birthday the next day, and she was going to buy me a present. Jessica is four months older than me and she always gets me something nice.

We were looking at some books and we saw this very chunky book, it had a red velvet cover with an embroidered gold thread all over, it was beautiful. It looked very old, in the corner is said, 'Written in 1721 by Albert Morris who died 21st March 1728'. I took a great big gulp, as that was my birthday.

That night as I fell asleep I couldn't stop thinking about the book. I imagined his face and what he would have been like. Then suddenly I was in 1721 and was watching Albert Morris writing a book in a big room with lots of books on the shelves. A candle was flickering on his desk. He was an old man with a long grey beard. I was trying not to be noticed when I fell over one of his books.

The next thing I knew was I was lying in hospital with a broken ankle!

Lucy Baker (11)
Snaith Primary School, Nr Goole

MY GHOST STORY

One day me and my friends heard all about a spooky house, so we all went to look around the house. When we got there the house had smashed windows and a creaky door.

When we were walking around the house the floorboards creaked, the wardrobes were full with witches clothes and vampires clothes. In nearly every cupboard there was a ghost. When we opened a cupboard door the ghosts jumped out at us.

In the kitchen all the food was rotten and all the pop was blood. When we ran the tap the water was all black. The ghosts always answered the door. Everyone was scared when they walked past the house.

Nobody wanted to have a look around the house but we were very brave to look around the house. We were not scared of the witches and the vampires or the ghosts.

One night the vampire went out and sucked blood out of people and the witches went out and cast spells on people but the ghost stayed at home just incase someone came to look at the house. The ghost had to open the door so the people could come in.

Daniel Hill (10)
Snaith Primary School, Nr Goole

Diary Of A Dog - Sally

April 21st 2002

It's Sunday today and you know what that means! You probably don't so I'll tell you. On Sundays I go to my grandma's while my mum, dad and Tim go off somewhere else. When they come back we have lunch. Me and my uncle Jacky pig whine to get food and in conclusion, we eat all the leftover chicken! I once ate some foil cos I was that hungry! We go there every Sunday, would you believe, it's not boring at all!

July 30th 2002

Tim's suddenly stopped going wherever he goes at 9 o'clock, so I've never got the house to myself! Before, I'd lounge about all day. Today is a happy day though, because it's walkies! We dogs enjoy our walkies. Oh the thrill of having the wind in your fur, the free earth below your paws, the excitement of trying to catch a stick while it is still in the air, being on the edge of running too fast and ending up rolling in a ball, tired, having ran through several holly bushes, rolling in a patch of mud and getting a very painful bang on the head by a gate. What bliss!

Tim Rooker (10)
Snaith Primary School, Nr Goole

A Day In The Life Of Gareth Gates

Wow! Ever since the hit TV show Pop Idol, my life has transformed. It has flipped over to become a wonderful new world that I could not even dream of.

When the show first hit the screens with I, Gareth Gates, on it, I had absolutely no idea I would be in the final two. But unfortunately I didn't win, the person who did win, William Young, deserved to win because he was older than me and much wiser too. Lots of people who starred in the show became instantly recognised and have lots of fans.

Anyway my job is to tell you about this fine, lovely day and what I did. First, I went to see Westlife in their studio for them to give me a few tips on how to perform to a live audience and how to keep calm. They say yoga is very good to keep you calm so if you want to become famous that's a tip. Then I went to the CD:UK music programme to perform to a live audience and the nation. Cat Deely, the presenter, is a really kind and generous person. The audience were really cheerful and shouty and all the girls were reaching out to me.

At around 2.30pm me and Will Young met in London's very own Internet Cafe for a chat on how we were enjoying being famous.

Not so long after that I was walking along London Bridge and a crowd of girls made a ring around me saying how much they love me and asking if they could have my autograph. That took up a lot of the day!

Soon after that I returned to my hotel knowing that tomorrow will be another long day just like today. That was my day.

Samantha West (10)
Snaith Primary School, Nr Goole

In Disneyland Paris

It was all of a sudden, we got to Discoveryland and saw the big ride called Space Mountain. It looked so frightening to me. The launching ramp was horizontal and when you got to the top of the ramp, it was so sudden but brilliant because you went vertical and then into a loop for a few seconds. Later you came to a three hundred and sixty degree spin and that was so cool.

We were still in Discoveryland, right next to Space Mountain, we were just going into Star Tours with our fastpass tickets, the fastpass tickets are so you don't have to queue for ages. The ride was a simulator but it actually felt like it was real because of the movement of the simulator and the graphics were brilliant.

All of us went to see the parade and Mickey and Minnie Mouse came past on a boat as well as Beauty and the Beast. It was so fancy and fantastic, how they set it out and put the parade together every day at the same time.

We went on a train and it took us all the way round the park. It was their 10th anniversary when we were there.

Oliver McArdle (11)
Snaith Primary School, Nr Goole

Rikkel Kierner

I was only five when my mum died. She died of cancer and after that my dad ran away and he never came back. He left me, Sara, Jenny, Lisa, Dave and Ian. Dave's the oldest and Ian is the youngest. I live in an orphanage and so does Ian but my brother and sisters went to live in houses. I took good care of my brother, I didn't want to lose him too.

One day I got really upset, I decided to run away, I went outside into the cold and something fell out of the bag, it was my mum's diamond necklace, I held it in my hand . . .

I suddenly started to feel dizzy, I was going round in circles, then bang! I had hit the ground. I was by the side of a shining lake. I went up to the lake, it was silent for a while but then my mum and dad came.
My mum said, 'You're with us Rikkel, you can live with us forever.'

I thought, I must be dead, and that's why I have to finish this story here. And if you ever meet Ian Kierner tell him Rikkel misses him.

Zoë Bakewell (11)
Snaith Primary School, Nr Goole

A Day In The Life Of Tibby

Hello I'm Tibby. I'm a cat. I have five pet humans but I won't go into detail about those messy things! By the way did you know that I am a princess! Anyway, I have just been prowling around the garden looking for mice but there was an annoyance. That cheeky stray that thinks he can go anywhere he likes has been in *my* garden, doing his business in my resting place, how rude! I couldn't put up with him any longer so I pounced on his back until he went straight out the gate! I would have fought him but I didn't want to get my itzy flitzy collar scratched!

I'm feeling very proud of myself now so I'm off for tea. My pets attend to my every need, in fact they are at my beck and call from 7am until 8.30pm, then hunting time begins! Recently I have fallen out with my pets for cutting down my favourite shady place but if I am desperate I could forgive them I suppose! *Yawn*! I'm tired now, I'm off to find myself a bed! No point you hanging around! Bye chums!

Faye Bowmer (11)
Snaith Primary School, Nr Goole

A DAY IN THE LIFE OF LITTLE MISS SUNSHINE

My name is Little Miss Sunshine, my best friends' names are Little Miss Tiny and Little Miss Topsy-Turvy, and they describe me as bright and bubbly.

I live at fifty-four Raindrop Road, Rainbowland. On a night I take a glass of warm milk and a hot water bottle up to my bedroom and climb into my red and yellow sun-shaped bed. Then I have a silent night's sleep.

In the morning I have a bowl of cornflakes and also a slice of toast with marmalade. Then after a while I go to see Little Miss Chatterbox. I intend to stay at Little Miss Chatterbox's house for about fifteen minutes, but normally I have to stay for about six hours. So I normally stay for dinner.

I think that this is lovely place to live in, and how the money grows on trees is fantastic, even though it did screw up Mr Sneeze's business in the bank.

The best thing about Rainbowland is that everything is so colourful especially the coloured birds, which are striped with the colours of the rainbow.

It's getting on for my bedtime now so I better be getting back, thank you for interviewing me, good night.

Poppy Robinson (11)
Snaith Primary School, Nr Goole

TRAPPED

'Hurry up Danielle,' Kimberley shouted.
Although Kimberley was small, she was a fast wriggler and could easily out wriggle Danielle.
'I'm going as fast as I can,' Danielle yelled back.

Danielle and Kimberley wriggled down to the sea to paddle, but as they started to swim there was a giant ripple followed by a wave. Everyone ran onto the sandy beach knocking down sandcastles and screaming, everyone except Kimberley and Danielle.

Danielle shouted for help, but it was too late because a giant orange tentacle had come up from the depths of the sea and taken the two girls under.

'Help!' Danielle tried to scream again but she hit her head hard on a rock and started to pass out.

An hour later Danielle and Kimberley woke up, at first they thought it was just a bad dream but when they looked around they realised it was real.

The two girls looked around and saw all sorts of amazing sea creatures, lobsters, crabs, eels, jellyfish and sea horses and then they finally saw it, the giant octopus which had dragged them underwater.

'What are you?' Kimberley asked the giant octopus.
'I am called Aqua Monster,' boomed the giant octopus. 'and you will make the perfect meal!' the giant octopus laughed.
'No! No!' they both yelled together. 'We're trapped!' and with that the two girls fainted.

Fifteen minutes later they woke up and found that they were above water, they looked down and saw they were lying on a dolphin.

'Hello you two girls,' said the dolphin. 'I see you are awake.'
'Yes, and thank you for rescuing us but how did you do it?' chorused Kimberley and Danielle.

'Simple really, just tied some seaweed to two of the bars and pulled them, I worked it out last week and I couldn't let you two be supper, now climb off my back because I can see some cameramen coming,' said the dolphin smiling.

The two girls wriggled across the beach burning their tummies on the sandy ground and smiled.
'Let's keep our underwater adventure to ourselves, as a secret,' Kimberley said squeezing salt water out of her long brown hair.
'Yes, or everyone will think we're mad.' replied Danielle.

So when the cameramen came they just told them that they were pushed underwater by a gigantic wave and rescued by two dolphins. The two girls had their names in the paper and were each awarded a medal for being brave.

'You know what Danielle,' Kimberley said, 'I quite liked that underwater adventure.'
'Me too!' smiled Danielle, and with that they jumped into the water with a splash and admired their fins.
'I love being a mermaid,' they said together and swam away reading the paper with the headline 'Mermaids spotted'.

Stephanie Hill (11)
Swineshead St Mary's Primary School, Boston